THE PERFORMANCE ILLUSION

CHAP CLARK

NAVPRESS
BRINGING TRUTH TO LIFE
NavPress Publishing Group
P.O. Box 35001, Colorado Springs, Colorado 80935

The Navigators is an international Christian organization. Jesus Christ gave His followers the Great Commission to go and make disciples (Matthew 28:19). The aim of The Navigators is to help fulfill that commission by multiplying laborers for Christ in every nation.

NavPress is the publishing ministry of The Navigators. NavPress publications are tools to help Christians grow. Although publications alone cannot make disciples or change lives, they can help believers learn biblical discipleship, and apply what they learn to their lives and ministries.

Library of Congress Catalog Card Number:
     93-7228
ISBN 08910-97406

Some of the anecdotal illustrations in this book are true to life and are included with the permission of the persons involved. All other illustrations are composites of real situations, and any resemblance to people living or dead is coincidental.

Clark, Chap, 1954-
     The performance illusion / Chap Clark.
          p.   cm.
     Includes bibliographical references.
     ISBN 0-89109-740-6
     1. Good works (Theology).   2. God—Love.
3. God—Worship and love.   4. Christian life—1960-
I.   Title.
BT773.C57   1993
234—dc20   93-7228
                                                                              CIP

Printed in the United States of America

FOR A FREE CATALOG OF
NAVPRESS BOOKS & BIBLE STUDIES,
CALL 1-800-366-7788 (USA)
or 1-416-499-4615 (CANADA)

CONTENTS

FOREWORD

There is a drivenness about the American people. It is nothing new. Alexis de Tocqueville saw it when he surveyed the citizens of our newly formed republic in the early nineteenth century. De Tocqueville attributed it to Americans lacking any clear system of assigned status. He saw us as a collection of individuals each of whom is trying to establish his or her own place in society through personal achievements. Since in the United States people are supposed to earn their places on the ladder of success, said de Tocqueville, no person is able to relax. Each and every one of us is expected to work day and night to improve his or her station in life. And every American, contended de Tocqueville, lives in fear of falling back.

Somehow we Christians believe that being caught up in the drive to achieve recognition and to obtain the symbols of success is something that we left behind when we committed ourselves to Christ. But few beliefs are further from the truth. We may even be sicker in this respect than the

5

rest of the world. The symbols of success may change, but Christians are even more plagued than others by anxieties concerning their performances in life.

For Christians the stakes are even higher than they are among secularists. Christians attach ultimate significance to their struggle to perform *par excellence*. We are constantly judging ourselves in negative ways because we fall short of expectation. We think our prayer life isn't good enough; or our Bible study is not consistent or deep enough; or we are not witnessing enough; or we are not loving enough.

There are no basic requirements of righteous achievement that must be met before we can be part of God's Kingdom. God is not some kind of transcendental skylock demanding a pound of flesh from those of us who find ourselves incapable of "paying up" what we think is required of us.

For many of us this is hard to grasp. But Chap Clark tells all of us who are dying from busyness, and who are stressed out by the anxieties of an achievement-oriented society, to lighten up. He tries to break through the illusions that our performance in every day life is what earns us the right to be loved by God.

"The love of God for each of us is an established reality that we have to accept, and their is nothing we can do to either add or subtract from it." Chap wants us to understand that and to bathe in the freedom that such good news can provide.

Through the biographical episodes he relates, he wants us to feel his own struggle to escape from the pressures of not feeling "good enough" or not feeling worthy of love and acceptance by God. But more than that, he wants us to learn how we can express a godlike unconditional love to those around us. He wants each of us to become a liberation theologian in the sense that each might become an agent of God, who frees people from the burdens that require them to be "peak performers" in all avenues of life.

A friend of mine recently had to resign from his position of leadership because of an extramarital affair. Behind all of his troubles, by his own admission, was a desire to find somebody who would worship him. He was looking for somebody who would praise him for his achievements and be ignorant of his shortcomings. Since his wife knew him too well to do that, he looked for someone else who would. And he succeeded—only to be destroyed in the process. Now he's trying to learn both from the Lord and from his faithful wife that he is loved anyway. He wants the joy that comes from being loved without achievement. And he is starting to sing, "Just As I Am."

Maybe this book will help some of the rest of us to sing that classic invitational hymn. And maybe we can learn before we do too much damage to ourselves and to those around us.

TONY CAMPOLO
Professor of Sociology
Eastern College
Saint Davids, Pennsylvania

ACKNOWLEDGMENTS

This book has been a gift to me from several different people. As I have read, researched, and written on the issue of performance we all struggle with, I have been continually reminded of how these friends have taught me what it means to live in freedom. There are many more friends who have made a lasting mark on me than I can list here. But these individuals have specifically written this book on my heart:

Dee, my wife, my friend. Thank you for teaching me how richly God can love through a person.

Mike and Karla Yaconelli, soul mates who have seen the best and the worst, and still love me unconditionally.

Henri J. M. Nouwen, a mentor and friend.

Sue Mosteller, a brilliant teacher whose gentleness and simplicity touched me.

The faculty, staff, and students of Denver Seminary, who are committed to keeping pace with the Spirit of God as we seek to influence our culture for Jesus Christ.

My parents, John and Gale Clark, and my in-laws, John and Jan Carlson, who have carried the weight of raising and loving two very strong-willed children named Dee and Chap for nearly four decades.

Friends and colleagues at Youth Specialties, especially Tic, Wayne, Duffy, Ridge, Ray, Noel, Doug, Denise, and Lauri. Thank you for providing a fellowship of friendship, which made the work all the more fun.

PREFACE

This book was hard to write. It began with a passion. Then, like other books, it continued with research, outlines, notes, and discussions. As issues began to take shape, ideas began to flow, and conversations intensified, it became a book I knew I had to write. But the more I got into the concepts of performance and freedom and grace and health, the more I realized that I needed to *read* this book before I could write it. And that is what happened.

I realized that God had been writing this book on my heart for twenty years. Like nothing else I have written, it is as much autobiography as "how-to." As you read you may see my tears dashed across the pages—for the most part they are tears of joy. I know that I have a long, long way to go to understand how performance driven I am, and how I rely on external forces to provide me with a sense of worth and meaning. But at least I am on the road, and I thank God for that.

If this book touches you, perhaps it will be because

you have developed the candid willingness that its content demands. Perhaps you have already faced, or are now facing, the issues of loneliness, frustration, and fear to which it speaks. But even if you have not entered those waters, I believe that at some point you will. So whatever your unique experiences, I encourage you to read on.

For those of you who are like me — scared of the future, nervous with the present, hoping that nobody will look deeply enough into your life to realize what a fraud you think you are — this book is for you. God has not abandoned us sinners, broken and unlovely as we may feel, and that is the good news we need to remember. This book is my gift to you, my fellow performer.

PART ONE

What's Gone Wrong?

Then Jesus said to the crowds and to his disciples:
"The teachers of the law and the Pharisees
sit in Moses' seat. So you must obey them
and do everything they tell you.
But do not do what they do, for they do not practice what
they preach. They tie up heavy loads
and put them on men's shoulders,
but they themselves are not willing to lift a finger
to move them. . . . Woe to you, teachers of the law and
Pharisees, you hypocrites! You shut the kingdom of heaven
in men's faces. You yourselves do not enter, nor will you
let those enter who are trying to."

MATTHEW 23:1-4,13-14

■■■■

Nothing less than life in the steps of Christ
is adequate to the human soul or the needs
of our world. Any other offer fails to do justice
to the drama of human redemption,
deprives the hearer of life's greatest opportunity,
and abandons this present life to the evil powers
of the age. The correct perspective is to see following Christ
not only as the necessity it is,
but as the fulfillment of the highest human
possibilities and as life on the highest plane.
It is to see, in Helmut Thielicke's words,
that "the Christian stands, not under the dictatorship
of a legalistic 'You ought,'
but in the magnetic field of Christian freedom,
under the empowering of the 'You may.'"

DALLAS WILLARD
The Spirit of the Disciplines

1

"I'VE BEEN HAD!"

W hat defines my value as a person? The clothes I wear, the friends I have — or maybe my accomplishments? Or, more to the point, *what makes me valuable?*

A friend of mine attended a junior high track meet to watch his daughter compete. It was an invitational with several schools, so there was a large crowd.

For the boys' mile race, ten young men anxiously lined up at the start. As soon as the gun sounded, they took off with the nervous energy of three-year-old thoroughbreds breaking from the gate. Soon the pack began to lose steam and settle into a more methodical pace. One heavyset boy fell back immediately, and it was soon obvious that this kid was no miler. He didn't even belong in the race.

Before the first lap had been completed this boy had fallen back nearly a hundred yards. At the half-mile, he was close to being lapped by the front runner. His peers in the crowd were watching him, and as early adolescents often do, began mercilessly taunting and laughing at the heavy youngster. Some even started yelling at him to drop out.

One woman standing in the middle of the crowd watched with particular intensity as the boy neared the end of his third lap, having been lapped by almost every other runner. With a mixture of desperation and disappointment she screamed out to him, "Johnny, run faster!!"

Johnny, run faster.

"Johnny, you idiot, what do you think you're doing? You're embarrassing me and making everyone else uncomfortable! You're fat and slow, and I want you to start performing like a runner—NOW!"

For a moment Johnny produced a slightly perceptible increase in speed and effort, but he was so discouraged by his inability to catch up that his pace became even more burdened, his posture more defeated.

ON THE RUN THROUGH LIFE

Now imagine that you are Johnny. Can you remember what it felt like growing up? Maybe it happened whenever your mom told you that you needed to be more active. Can you hear her voice, even now?

"You don't have enough friends. Why don't you get out there and meet some people—the right kind of people? Sign up for a sport," she says.

So you do, but the only sport that will take you is the track team, and they only have room with the milers. So you try, because you know deep down that your parents want you to succeed at something, and you never had much of a chance to be involved in any other sport. *Who knows?* you think. *After all, maybe I'll be good at track.*

So you work out with the team. You train. You run. No one really talks to you much, but that's okay, because for once you're part of something. And the big day comes, and you're facing the first meet.

You know you're in trouble when the other guys ask

you with a smirk if you really intend to go through with it, "You're not gonna run, are you, Johnny?" As you line up for the gun your heart is pounding, wondering what in the world you're doing out there. The gun fires. You're off.

This is fun! you think, as you round the first turn with a burst of energy. *I can keep up with these guys!* But all too soon you realize with horror that you started out at far too fast a pace. Your heart pumping, your head pounding, you realize that you're falling back fast.

Now all you can think of is how ridiculous you look, trying to be a runner—and in front of all these people. The others fly by you. A few laugh, but most just pass, pretending that you don't even exist.

Then, out of the stands you hear your mom, the one voice you need above all others to shout encouragement. . . .

"Johnny, run faster!!"

It's all you can do to stay on the track and finish the race.

"Johnny, run faster!!"

I am Johnny. I'm not terribly overweight, and I didn't run track in junior high. I even had friends, and when my folks did come to the games, they generally kept silent or shouted some encouragement. But none of that really matters.

I am Johnny.

I've spent most of my life putting on a predesignated uniform, going through my exercises, and running around somebody else's track, on a course I didn't really like—all in the hope that it would somehow make me feel valuable. I have been involved in sports, music, and drama. I have often been popular, successful, and a leader in various groups. But I can still feel myself running, watching people pass me and hearing them laugh and jeer as they race past. Often, out of the stands I hear the voices of those closest to me relationally, telling me how to achieve a better finish in the race. I am tired, I am afraid, and I feel alone.

CAUGHT ON THE PERFORMANCE TREADMILL

Jesus Christ said, "Come to me, you who are weary, and I will give you rest." These words sound so inviting, and ring so true. Why is it that so many in the Christian community have yet to find that rest?

Why is that so many of us hear God saying "Johnny, run faster!!" instead of "I will give you rest?"

In search of the answer to that question, I invite you to walk with me through the complex maze of the human heart. As we ask how and why we are so imprisoned by this need to perform, I hope you will discover that there is a place of refuge from the forces that burden you. I believe that the more you understand what has led you to this place, and the more you reflect on the *true* character of the God you have sought all these years, the more you will be able to step off the performance treadmill.

My personal Christian experience began when I was sixteen. I was so attracted to God's words and to His compassion that I responded with great zeal and passion. I wanted to be loved, to be free, and to be taken seriously for who I was. When I first heard this message, it was like the sky being opened. I felt ready to live life as I was created.

I did what those who were called "Christians" were expected to do, usually with pretty good success. I talked about Jesus to my friends and family, turning off and even hurting a few in the process. I got involved in church youth groups and choir tours. I even got rebaptized "right."[1] I went to camp; I served with missionaries; I went to conferences, Bible studies, and classes. I prayed, studied, and memorized the Scriptures. During those years (and mostly ever since), especially in high school, I lived according to the external expectations of my Christian world.

But I didn't feel very free. In fact, to be honest, those years increased my identification with Johnny. I felt guilty about my failings and shortcomings before I met Jesus, but nothing like I experienced afterward. Guilt took on a whole new meaning for me. Not only did I have to worry about my own legitimate failures, shortcomings, and hurts done to others, I now had to be constantly concerned that I was displeasing my God.

Despite what I was hearing about the Christian life, my relationship with the church reduced neither my guilt nor my frustration at my inability to perform properly. Because of my lack of consistent performance in what I perceived to be the norms of the Christian faith, my guilt actually *increased*. As hard as I tried, I couldn't live up to the expectations of the Christian community. I *tried* to pray regularly, because I knew that was what a Christian did, but my prayers lacked authenticity and power. I read the Bible, usually because it was a means of preparation for a meeting or talk, but it rarely touched me. I talked to others about Christ, but only when it was safe or proper, and then mostly to those who were already sympathetic.

For many years, although I placed great importance on my relationship to Jesus Christ, I was convinced that God was deeply disappointed in me. How *could* He be pleased with me, when I was such a failure?

This message was ingrained in me from my earliest days of faith. The year after I had expressed my desire to follow Jesus I went on a church trip with a friend from school. While on the bus I acted my age—adolescent—and got a bit rowdy with a few guys. I was soon singled out as a troublemaker and was loudly and publicly reprimanded with the words, "If *Jesus* were here, how would you feel?" I was told in no uncertain terms that if Jesus *were* alive and active, He certainly wouldn't approve of roughhousing. The message came through that if God were here in the flesh, watch out, fellas—He's gonna get ya!

In the environment I grew up in, Jesus was a God to be worshiped from afar—but for heaven's sake don't let Him see you fail! Second Corinthians 5:14 (NASB) became the verse that summed up my life as a believer—"For the love of Christ controls [me]." My Americanized and adolescent theology interpreted this to mean that *my love for Jesus Christ was what produced the valid and "fruitful" Christian experience.* God had done His part. He made me in His image, He lost me due to my own sin, and He came to earth to die so that I might once again have life so long as I followed His laws as He originally intended. He was risen—and I could see Him standing there with arms folded, brow furrowed, His job now to see whether I would be obedient. My job was to love Jesus, which would "compel" me to live for Him.

I was a Christian caught on the performance treadmill.

LEARNING TO DANCE

Author and lecturer Brennan Manning once saw a bumper sticker that said, "Jesus loves you: everyone else thinks you're a dork!" This Jesus who loves me is bound by His character to love. He loves me not because He's interested in me or because He is pleased with me, but because He's supposed to—that's His job! But so much of the Christian training and teaching I'd received over the years had me convinced that deep down inside I was an embarrassment to God.

One day, like a flash of lightning across a blackened sky, I saw the real meaning of those words in 2 Corinthians, "the love of Christ controls me." I realized that Paul wasn't talking about my love for Jesus as the motivating factor in the Christian experience. He was declaring that it was *Jesus' love for me* that gave meaning and purpose to life. Jesus was the focus, not me! I was incapable of love, but He was infinitely capable to make me a lover. I was selfish, yet He had the ability to help me rise above my self-centered nature. I knew then that Jesus Christ was alive and active and so I didn't have to worry—for His power was the catalyst that would bring me safely through the failures and disappointments of my life.

Mike Yaconelli, my friend and mentor, once preached a sermon on the essence of the Christian life, using the imagery of dancing with Jesus. (I know that there are some who struggle with the issue of dancing, but let's for a moment see dancing as a biblical expression of celebration, as Psalm 150:4 exclaims — "praise him with tambourine and dancing.") Mike quoted Sue Monk Kidd, in her rich book *When the Heart Waits:*

> Delight [in our relationship with Christ] can become a way of life, a way of journeying. There's a saying, "Religion is not to be believed, but danced." I like this idea, for it shifts the emphasis from our endless pursuit of religious knowledge back to the dimension of *living* our religion in such a way that it becomes a dance, a celebration in which we open our arms and say yes to life.[2]

One of the most memorable experiences of my junior high years was learning how to ballroom dance.[3] The teacher (who in those days was referred to as "the gym coach") was responsible for teaching the seventh grade class of Cloonan Junior High School how to understand and appreciate ballroom dancing in two or three days. Our gym coach had a flat-top haircut, spandex shorts, rotund physique, and a gruff exterior — but inside he was all bull elephant!

Coach began by lining us up across the length of the gym, guys on one side and girls on the other. He pointed to the large blackboard on the wall, on which he had scrawled a few footprints, numbers, and dotted lines. As he explained the beauty of ballroom dancing to us, he said, "This is all there is to it. Look at the board. You put your left foot here [pointing with a long stick] on one, your right foot here on two, and so on. Any idiot can do it. Now, ready. . . ." As he counted off we were to practice the steps as shown on the board. "One, two, three, *slide* . . . one, two, three, *slide*. . . ."

After trying to put the steps to music that was drowned out by the nervous laughter of the class and scratches on the record, we were told to pair up boy/girl. This was fascinating, because he didn't give us any logistical instructions for how to do this—except to hurry. And most of the girls averaged a foot taller than most of the boys. As Coach played the record and exhorted us to "dance!" he continued to harangue us for our failure to get it right!

To this day I hate ballroom dancing. It was mechanical, awkward, and embarrassing. The girl I was paired with didn't want to be with me, and the feeling was mutual. The point of the lesson was to instill a love for the historical beauty of this type of social interaction. But because of the messenger and the way the message was delivered, it inspired the opposite result.

As I look back on the Christian education and training I have received, I think one of my biggest stumbling blocks was that few told me how wonderful it is to dance with Jesus. I heard that in order to perform the dance of the Christian life, there were certain steps that I had to learn, memorize, and perfect. Without them, I would never be able to dance. Prayer, Bible study, church attendance, service, giving, verbally "witnessing" to others—these were the "one, two, three" steps that were essential to master before I could actually dance.

Sometimes the messengers were gentle and kind, but more often those entrusted with teaching the dance were harsh, arrogant, and authoritative. It was implied that I could never measure up to their ability to dance. And so I watched my feet, trying to get the steps down. I was learning not for the enjoyment of the dance, but because it was expected of me. How miserable I felt when I compared my own stumbling efforts with those who seemed to be able to do it naturally.

Too many of us have missed the beauty and essence of the dance because we're so worried what others are thinking of our performance. We have absorbed the myth that the steps of religious performance are of primary concern to God. Yes, dancing is performing. But when a dance is an expression of a life free from an anxious, guilt-ridden compulsion to be good, it is a thing of beauty.

I believe that the biblical message frees us of the need to perform in order to experience the joy and wonder of dancing with God. As we dance, every tear, failure, and blemish is swept away by the majesty of the dance. We are transformed, not by learning the steps or showing off the gracefulness of our performance, but by the intimate reality of touching, feeling, and moving with a Lord who leads with laughter. As we dance, every area of our lives is renewed, for we see life as it was meant to be seen. We are free to live without craving the approval of others, without desperately searching for significance, without even caring how we look—for we are the beloved of the Most High, and we are His delight.

He has reached out His scarred, gentle hand to me, a simple, plain, and lonely onlooker to the great dance of life and whispered, "Would you like to dance with me?"

He knows my fears. "I'm so clumsy . . . there are others so much better than I am . . . I'm afraid I will let you down. . . ."

"Come dance with me," He insists, "and I will teach you how to dance. You were made to dance. Come dance and laugh and twirl and shout with Me!"

Come dance with the King!

2

IN THE NAME OF LOVE

W hen I was about four years old, my grandmother gave me a book called *Love Is a Feeling to Be Learned.* I remember nothing about the book, but the title has always stuck with me.

I suppose that's because everywhere I look the message is the same: love is a feeling. It is fickle; it comes and it goes like the wind. It works only when both people's feelings happen to line up at the same time in the same place. And even then it isn't very trustworthy, for at any moment something could change and love would vanish. Most of what I see in the media and hear in the songs is that love is based more on what I want and feel than what the object of my love wants or feels.

There is something artificial, even evil, about this cultural concept of love. Relationships are increasingly fragile, and many are hurt as a result. But we still lift high the ideal of love as the ultimate solution to our problems.

Those of us caught by the need to perform are especially

susceptible to this illusion. We search for a place of safety where we won't feel the need to be good enough or talented enough or consistent enough to be loved and accepted. We long for a love that can free us from our desperate need to live up to others' expectations of us. But more often than not, our experience of love is woefully lacking.

Love is one of the most misused and misunderstood terms in our language. "Tough love" can describe harsh discipline and even relational rigidity. "Puppy love" primarily refers to a young person's immature and usually groundless romantic feelings. "God's love" (frequently referred to with the New Testament term *agape,* a Greek word describing God's design for relationships) is usually defined as "unconditional" —but most teachers quickly temper this by adding a list of qualifiers intended to protect God from what one writer called "sloppy agape."[1]

The key word in each of these short phrases remains something of an enigma to our culture. Is the essence of love discipline? Romance? Unconditional acceptance despite behavior and without relational consequences? Is it reliable, or does it inevitably fade or change? Does it simply describe a propensity toward something, as in "I love that new Lexus"? Or does the concept of "love" have some objective content to which our lonely and floundering culture can cling?

WHEN LOVE IS TIED TO ACCOMPLISHMENT

During a discussion with a few acquaintances at a recent conference, the conversation got around to our families. One young woman with us was asked about her background, and her story grabbed us.

Elizabeth was raised in what she had always felt was a "loving" home environment. The family was very close, or so it seemed. The dinner table was a bit of a cultural rarity in that it was the occasion for family chatter, catching up, and discussion. When someone was involved in an activity such as sports or a dramatic presentation, both parents — if not the entire family — were sure to be in attendance. And they were an active family: nearly every night and weekend was filled with one or more commitments. But everyone was supportive, and Elizabeth's parents were glad to sacrifice, for they were committed to the kids.

The older Elizabeth got, the more she began to resent her parents, especially her father. She could not understand it, but there was definitely a block developing, and this deeply troubled her. She knew her father loved her; in fact, he told her so several times a day. She knew he was for her and was her "biggest fan," because not only did he come to everything she was involved with, he often coached or assisted. He was warm, he listened to her, and he desired to spend a lot of time with her. But still something was wrong, and Elizabeth could not put her finger on it.

As the years passed, Elizabeth's silent resentment began to make itself heard in subtle ways. At first she would lie to her parents about her activities so they would miss events. Then she dropped out of an activity or two that she knew her father especially enjoyed. After some confrontation and heated discussion, she began to cut as many emotional ties with her father as possible.

Today, in her late twenties, Elizabeth speaks with bitterness and anger about her family. She is determined not to "stifle" her kids as she perceived had been done to her. "They will be able to live their own lives, and I will not interfere with them at all."

Listening to this young woman I had just met, I was sad for both her and her folks. She kept saying how much they loved her, and yet she had felt "smothered" to the point of completely turning her back on them.

"Can love smother?" someone in the group asked her.

"The way *my* dad loved me sure did!" she testily replied. "I didn't mind him coming to my events, games, and plays when I was growing up, and I actually *liked* the fact that he was constantly cheering for my friends and me.

But I hated going home with him later."

"Was he critical?"

"Not really," she went on, "at least not very often. He was usually very complimentary, in fact. I remember his most typical line was, 'Honey, I sure was proud when you made that score (or sang that song, or hit that ball). I sure love you!'" I got to *hate* him telling me how much he loved me when I did well, because I felt like if I was ever to *not* do well, *where would I be then?*"

Like a warm summer day chilled by a sudden storm, the conversation ceased. Large tears dropped from Elizabeth's eyes as she excused herself from the table.

We sat in the silence of our own private worlds, listening to the tapes of our own history. As some started to open up and we again began to share, each of us discovered that Elizabeth was not alone.

It is obvious that we have all been profoundly influenced by our families. What is not obvious, however, is how even the most positive experiences may have contributed to a deeply imbedded expectation and a perceived need to perform.

A family in which the father is always present, loving, and fun may also spawn innocent comments like, "You're so smart, you always get straight A's! I really love you!" Inadvertently, a message is communicated that perpetuates the performance ethic. Translated, the recipient may hear that message as, "You performed well, and I expect you always to perform well, and because of that I love you." Even the most well-intentioned family can focus more on the deed of accomplishment than the character of the person when giving praise and encouragement.

If love means anything, it means I accept you as you are, not as I want you to be. We all need to experience the love that is not tied to our accomplishments, no matter how lofty they may be. Unfortunately for many of us, even parents seem to miss this. Praise for a good performance is good, healthy, and necessary for development, but it must never be connected to an ultimate sense of one's value in the family.

For example, if Elizabeth's father were confronted with the consequences of his comments, he would mostly likely respond, "I *never* intended to communicate that! There is *no question* that I love my kids. I would love them even if they *weren't* stars." But all it took was his choice of words to send his little girl a vastly different message.

Historically speaking, excellence in performance has been a motivating factor in raising kids since the Stone Age. And it has been applied to just about every aspect of their lives. The proverbial Little League coach, for example, is "just another dad" willing to spend the time it takes to keep a bunch of seven-to-twelve-year-olds from killing each other with an extremely dangerous projectile while instilling in them teamwork and commitment. The institution of youth sports, however, does not typically attract leaders who are simply filling a slot. Their ranks swell with former high school athletes who remember their coach as doing them the favor of their lives by creating in them that most necessary of athletic commodities—the thirst for victory! For this type of coach the best way to motivate children is to let them know that the better they perform the more valuable they will be to the team—and the illusion continues. . . .

I currently have two boys in Little League, seven and ten years old. One is just learning the difference between catching and throwing, and the other thinks, eats, and sleeps baseball. During an average summer week Dee and I will attend six games, not including rain outs. I go as often as possible; I can even say that I *enjoy* watching my boys play.

My struggle with this issue of performance has caused me to spend a great deal of time in reflection while watching these games. My younger son, Robbie, who has just taken up the sport, appears to need very little personal success. The level of competition is not very fierce, his coaches get more exasperated than angry at the performance (or lack of it) of his seven-and-eight-year-old teammates, and his friends don't seem to make a big issue out of who's good and who isn't.

Last week, for example, Robbie's inaccurate throw on the last play of the game caused his team to lose a tight ball game. As I approached him I was concerned to see him crying but relieved by his explanation: "We lost, Dad!" He had no sense of personal failure or crisis of self-worth because of his error. He was just sad and disappointed that his team had lost. For me this was a cause to celebrate, for part of growing up is learning how to handle the inevitable disappointments of competition—and there is no escaping competition in this world. But Robbie was not personally hurt, defeated, or depressed . . . not yet, anyway.

I have a standard line when introducing my eldest son: "He's named after a great American!" I proudly assert. Chappie lives in a completely different world. When he misses even one pitch, his coach yells out to him, "Watch the ball!" or "Keep your head in!" or "Protect the plate!" With every swing, there's a comment.

And here I am, his father—the one in the best position to continually remind him that he is fantastic as he is, not as he performs—yelling out to him right along with his coach. Now my son can add another worry to the list—the speed of a hard object coming right for him, several friends watching to see if he's going to blow it, a few grown men providing him with contradictory and ominous instructions, a catcher telling him how bad a player he really is. Now his father is telling him he'll *really* be a neat kid if he'll just get a hit.

It took a good friend watching Chappie and listening to me to make that observation, and I am not quite over it. Here I was writing a book on performance, while laying the performance ethic on my own kid as he stood at the plate.

Perhaps you never played sports. Or perhaps you were so good at sports it never seemed to bother you what others thought of your rare failure experiences. But most of us have been so indoctrinated with this view of performance that it has penetrated to our very core. Although it seems obvious that we all need to be loved no matter how well we do in life, somehow we're losing the battle when it comes to how we treat each other — whether in our families, churches, schools, or even with our best friends.

Author and speaker Steve Brown says that his inability to deal with this contradiction of knowledge and life has led him to the following conclusion when he is gathered with a group of adults in a social setting: "We are all sick. The only difference is I know it and they don't!"[2] This is the first step in defeating the power of the performance illusion: recognizing that the performance messages are all around us, and realizing how even the most subtle can remind us of our struggle to prove ourselves.

IS "EXCELLENCE" ALL THAT MATTERS?

Our culture hammers home from many different angles that the ultimate goal for us all is to pursue — if not achieve — "excellence." Both Christian and general bookstores are filled with volumes that seduce us into believing there really is such an objective reality known as "excellence." It sounds so good, doesn't it? So lofty, so moral.

Yet who defines "excellence"? Who has "arrived"? Who keeps their eyes on the ball well enough that they hit it with power, every time?

No one does, not even the best. And that is precisely the problem. We have been harnessed to the treadmill of success and achievement based on our performance, and even our family sometimes turns up the dial.

Although this trend has been true for the last generation or two, it is increasingly magnified as the years go by. The lifestyle of today's culture has led us even deeper into the excellence trap.

A friend of mine was speaking at a parenting conference in rural Northern California. After his presentation a woman approached him with the following question: "My daughter is so busy, so stressed out, that I am afraid for her.

She is constantly worrying—about her clothes, her hair, her car, her boyfriends. She is a real perfectionist, and I don't know what to do. Is there any way I can help her?"

This woman was attractive in the same way that one would describe a high-class mannequin as attractive. Her clothes were stylish and expensive, her hair was carefully coiffured, her makeup was a bit overdone, and her sun-lamp tan was seasonably out of place. Her abundant jewelry was noticeably missing from her left ring finger, which was quickly explained by her assertion that she was a single parent.

With genuine compassion for this woman, my friend hesitated slightly before he said, "Tell you what. Next week surprise your daughter by picking her up during the middle of the day. Don't wear any makeup, don't even wash your hair. Throw on a pair of old jeans, a T-shirt and a baseball cap, and have her change into the same thing when you get her. Drive to the coast and check into a cheap motel near the beach. Spend two or three days taking walks, going to movies, riding horses, and just playing together outside. And don't just say 'I love you,' but hold her hand, stroke her hair, and listen to her."

The look on this woman's face during and following his reply indicated that she wasn't sure whether to be angry or offended or both. She knew, however, that *this* man did not understand, not for one minute! She was so wrapped up in her own pursuit of external beauty and "excellence" that she could not see how much more there was to life.

Ann Landers describes what is happening in today's families:

> The moral fiber of family life is coming apart at the seams because there's nobody home. Parents are not spending enough time with their children. They can't. The rat race is highly competitive, and children aren't valued the way they once were. Children were considered at least as important as a career. But no longer

is this true. The career gets the quality time, and the kids get what's left over.[3]

In the name of love parents try to build a home and a career "for the children." But sadly, all too often the reality is what Landers laments. Career gets the time, the energy, the focus. Why? Because that is where the parents get their desperately needed strokes of value and affirmation. They love their kids, but are so personally committed to being the best, the most successful, and the wealthiest that they leave their kids behind.

Sometimes parents virtually give up and turn over their children to be raised by "professionals." They want their kids to have all the advantages for competing in the world. Otherwise, they fear, their kids won't "make it" when it's time for them to perform. I recently ran across this ad in *Sunset* magazine for a boarding school:

> Why board your child?
>   —a safe, supportive environment . . .
>   —establish strong study skills . . .
>   —a balanced, structured program . . .
>   —prepare your child for life . . .
> A good 3rd-8th grade boarding program is hard to find!

Third grade? *Third grade?* I'm sorry if I am about to step on toes, but I cannot imagine a parent sending a nine-year-old child off to boarding school just so he can obtain "a safe, supportive environment."

One of the current trends hitting education circles is the movement to foster healthy self-esteem in students. School districts across the country are spending thousands of dollars trying to train their teachers in how to instill worth in kids—some of whom have no other place to learn it. But without a moral or philosophical basis for self-esteem, a societal theory of "values-neutral education" instead creates confusion about self-worth.

Consider, for example, the teacher who feels that the best way to enhance students' self-esteem is to push them to achieve their "academic potential." So her grading scale is tougher for certain kids than it is for others, creating for some students the constant pressure to fulfill some nebulous but highly expected level of potential.

I saw this firsthand when my oldest son's fourth-grade teacher refused to give him an A in spelling until he got 100 percent correct. In the trimester grade conference, my wife and I watched our son's shoulders droop when she told him that his grade of B minus—based on a 94 percent average in spelling—still left him far short of his potential. He knew very well that other students in his class with a lower percentage received an A for their work. This experience did cause him to work all the harder, but his motive was to prove to this teacher that he *was* valuable and smart, thus perpetuating in his impressionable young mind that unless you reach someone else's mark, you are nothing.

In the name of love, teachers, coaches, parents, bosses, and even friends put pressure on us to constantly improve and seek excellence. In the name of love, our society grades and tests and scores and evaluates and stratifies until we feel worthwhile only when (and if) we perform up to our "potential"—whatever that may be. In the name of love, we have been taught that we are not genuinely valuable until we perform as we are told . . . and so we keep running and swinging and jumping, always trying harder, all the while pleading for someone to stop the treadmill and let us rest.

But authentic love does not attach performance strings. Authentic love can overcome this ethic of success that drives us as a culture.

THE ONLY KIND OF LOVE THAT FREES US

While in seminary I was involved in an outreach ministry called Young Life, an organization committed to loving and sharing the gospel with young people. One girl in our group was president of her sophomore class, a 4.0 student, popular and attractive.

During the summer between her sophomore and junior years, however, Renee decided to abandon everything she had valued, and basically went crazy. She quickly got involved with the local drug crowd and experimented with dangerous narcotics. She sought one-night sexual encounters and had an abortion, not even knowing (and apparently not caring) who the father was. Though raised in a church-going home environment by parents who loved her, she treated them with as much hate and malice as she could. By the middle of the next year, she had effectively dropped out of school, and of life.

As a friend of the family, I was asked to house-sit one weekend while the parents were away. Friday night at about two a.m. I received a call telling me where I could pick Renee up; she was too drunk to walk, they said. When I finally got her home and put to bed, I was livid. I felt that she knew better, and had simply made the decision not only to mess up her own life, but to bring everybody else down with her—including me.

As I walked into my bedroom, tired, angry, and frustrated, I noticed on the desk a framed, hand-written poem. It was written from her father's perspective:

> I have a daughter 17
>> When she lies to me . . . I love her.
>> When she disappoints me . . . I love her.
>> When she doesn't live up to my expectations . . .
> I love her.
>> When she reflects poorly on my name . . . I
> love her.
>
>> "Now I can understand how when she pleases
> you . . . and obeys you . . . and fulfills you . . . ,"
> you say.

But that's not what I'm talking about.
It's when she does none of these things . . . I
love her
AND for a very simple reason:

I'm her father . . . and she's my child.[4]

Nearly fifteen years later, she has returned to both her parents and her Lord.

Can you trace the roots of performance back to those who most influenced you? Were there individuals in your life who seemed to encourage you and like you regardless of how well you performed, behaved, or fit in? This is the kind of love that frees us—the *only* kind of love that can liberate us. We all desperately need to be loved without any strings attached, but parental love alone can never fully meet this need.

3

"IF THEY COULD SEE ME NOW"

"If they could see me now, that little gang of mine. . . ."
This advertising jingle was played year after year in the hopes that the North American public might be convinced to take a very expensive cruise vacation. The hook, or the appeal, of the ad goes something like this: "Wouldn't it be great to tell your friends and neighbors that *you* went on a cruise? You can make sure that you are more loved and respected just by joining us for three to ten days. . . ."

Few ads can stand up to logical analysis. Yet advertisers spend a lot of money to get us to buy one product over another, or to purchase something we don't even need. And it works: the advertising industry controls much of our lives.

Charles Barkley, professional basketball star with the Phoenix Suns, made this statement to *People* magazine:

I have a sneaker deal myself, but I don't understand why people would buy one sneaker endorsed by one player over the other. Kids idolize professional

athletes, which is wrong in itself, and they just copy
what they're wearing. I think one of the problems
we have in today's society is that it's the parents'
job to be role models. To kids that idolize me, I tell
them don't do so just because I can dribble a basketball—that's really sick.[1]

It *is* sick, but that hasn't stopped the advertising industry from continuing to push lies on us. As powerful as it
is, however, Madison Avenue is only the tip of the cultural
iceberg. Our society constantly barrages us with false messages. The greatest deception is the subtly presented yet
overpowering message that we live in an open, liberalized,
and pluralistic society in which the only important value
is self-autonomy. In this message, the individual reigns
supreme, as long as what he or she does doesn't interfere
with someone else's freedom.

This philosophy sounds fair, yet it is contradicted by
other messages society sends us. Our culture is like a tidal
wave of silent values that tell us over and over again how
impotent, unattractive, and insignificant we are. We can't
read the newspaper, flip through a magazine, watch television, or see a movie without being reminded of how little
we matter in this huge, complex world.

Whether by media design or through societal evolution,
our culture has drastically advanced our need to stay on the
performance treadmill. We have been sold a bill of goods we'll
be paying for in generations to come. This takes the form of
four major areas in which the world has enslaved us: (1) it has
set impossible standards, (2) it has sought to bring conformity
and uniformity to the masses, (3) it has deified the myth of
success, and (4) it has elevated busyness over godliness.

OUR CULTURE SETS IMPOSSIBLE STANDARDS

Michelle Pfeiffer, popular star of such films as *Batman
Returns* and *Russia House*, was featured on the cover of

Esquire magazine's December 1990 edition with the headline: "What Michelle Pfeiffer Needs . . . Is Absolutely Nothing." The cover photo pictured the beautiful and sensual Michelle Pfeiffer throwing her head back with abandon, as if to say, "Just look at how beautiful I am. I am a work of art."

Women all across North America were drawn to this cover in near record numbers. As they gazed in envy at the beauty of Michelle Pfeiffer and read the headline, they were led to think, "Michelle needs absolutely nothing, she is beautiful just the way she is!" The message came through loud and clear: "See this? *This* is beauty! *This* is what it means to be attractive. Now go look in the mirror. How do you personally measure up? Pretty shabby, huh? Better do something about it, because you aren't even close to being presentable!"

When I saw the cover I was both shocked and saddened, for Michelle Pfeiffer is no more beautiful in the eyes of God than Mother Teresa, Whoopi Goldberg, or the cashier behind the fast-food counter. Although the cover does not overtly devalue "ordinary" women, the statement it makes is undeniable.

I felt much better, however when I saw that the editors of *Redbook* had done a follow-up story on this cover in their January 1991 issue. They had discovered that Diane Scott Associates had sent *Esquire* a bill for the touch-up they did on the Michelle Pfeiffer cover. Apparently she needed more than the headline stated. Michelle's photo needed $1,525 of remedial work to "clean up complexion, soften eye lines, soften smile line, add color to lips, trim chin . . . adjust color and add hair on top of head." *No wonder the Michelle Pfeiffer on this cover is so beautiful,* I thought. *She doesn't exist! This cover is a lie!*

The performance treadmill keeps us running after artificial standards for how we *look* as well as what we *do*. But we don't reject these false messages. Most of us just keep trying. Mike Yaconelli, cofounder of Youth Specialties, commented on this sad reality:

A recent study was made with the American people. They were asked, "How might you fulfill your potential as a human being?" Here were the top two answers "I would be rich. I would be thin."

That's it? Those are the *top two answers* that define how Americans understand their value as a human being? Greed is okay, apparently, as long as it isn't fattening.

Isn't that incredible? Nothing about being a better person, being a person who could help people, being a person who could make a difference in the world. Nope. Just make my body thin. Is it any wonder that a survey of five hundred children in elementary school found that half the girls thought they were overweight and 31 percent of the ten year olds said they "felt fat," though only 15 percent were actually heavier than the norm? Is it any wonder that the new disorder psychologists are watching rise is what they call body dysmorphic disorder . . . in layman's terms . . . imagined ugliness. What is the obvious cause? Psychologists call it the "contrast effect." That means when we compare our real bodies to the bodies we see in advertisements and the media, we end up with a distorted view of our own bodies.

An ad appeared in numerous magazines recently that showed a beautiful young model in a bathing suit with the headline: "There are some things in life you just can't change. Your looks used to be one of them." So now we have all received the encouraging news that we don't have to look like this . . . we can fix it . . . because plastic — excuse me, *cosmetic* — surgery is now within reach of the middle class. Is it any wonder that so many young people are having difficulty with who they are? Is it any wonder that many of our young people have grown up being intimidated by a culture that says you are how you look?[2]

The first standard by which people usually judge us is how we look. But thanks to the power of the media, almost all of us find ourselves on the losing end of this struggle to fit in—whether because of our weight, our facial features, our hair, our race, the clothes we wear, or the car we drive. And so the performance treadmill moves faster as we try to keep up with the images that constantly remind us of how much we lack.

OUR CULTURE ENFORCES CONFORMITY AND UNIFORMITY

Although it can be argued that one of society's most basic roles is to ensure conformity to its ethos, in North American culture we have been pushed too far. From the educational system to the media's pervasive influence, there is presently very little room for one to choose to look, think, and live differently.

Christians rightly attempt to battle this tendency. But in resisting society's attempts to put them in a box, they may find themselves boxed in by the church as well. Many in the Christian community have reduced the struggle to resist social pressures to a black-and-white conflict between two distinct entities, the "world" and the "church." Consequently, many believers have felt shoved into somebody else's ideological box, whether in regard to political views on war and capital punishment, education, or even what kind of music they listen to. For these believers, it seems that choice has been virtually eliminated from the equation.

The last few years I have been trying to let go of my guilt and live out what I believe to be true about life. I'm not talking about immorality, disobedience, or anything that would violate divine or human moral codes. I'm just trying to live as one who is free to make decisions based on who I am in Christ, and on the highest principle given to me, love, instead of living from a guilt-ridden desire to please everyone else around me. I believe that this is the call of the followers of Jesus Christ. But the more I have searched, the more opposition I have experienced—however veiled or subtle. It's hard to stand upright with confidence in this world. It's easier simply to give in to the pressure around us, jump on the treadmill, and perform for all those voices of authority that seek to control our lives.

The individual is so mistrusted in our society that most of us wonder if we actually know what *we* think or want or feel. Where is the joy of discovery, the wonder of interaction, and the freedom to walk with Jesus in community with others without being afraid of exploring a thought?

Thomas Merton defined the problem of conformity in this way:

> The modern child may early in his or her existence have natural inclinations toward spirituality. The child may have imagination, originality, a simple and individual response to reality and even a tendency to moments of thoughtful silence and absorption. All these tendencies, however, are soon destroyed by the dominant culture. The child becomes a yelling, brash, false little monster, brandishing a toy gun or dressed up like some character he has seen on television. His head is filled with inane slogans, songs, noises, explosions, statistics, brand names, menaces and cliches. Then, when the child gets to school, he learns to verbalize, rationalize, to pace, to make faces like an advertisement, to need a car and, in short, to go through life with an empty head conforming to others, like himself, in togetherness.[3]

We must rediscover the joy and wonder of walking as free men and women—knowing that with freedom comes responsibility, but also great power to live, as Larry Crabb has said, from the inside out.

OUR CULTURE PERPETUATES
THE MYTH OF SUCCESS

During the 1992 Summer Olympics, an American super-heavyweight wrestler was expected to fare well against the rest of the world in his division. Maybe it wouldn't be a gold medal, but he hoped to get the silver. During one difficult match, with his wife and six-year-old daughter looking on, he lost in overtime. As his wife attempted to comfort the little girl, the NBC cameras provided the country with a close-up of his daughter in tears.

Later that night during the wrap-up show, Dick Enberg made this observation while we watched the little girl cry: "At her age, daddies aren't supposed to lose."

In North America, we have been raised with the myth that says *you can be and do whatever you set your mind to.* The idea that every opportunity for material, social, and emotional success waits for any person willing to do what it takes has been so ingrained in our way of life that we scarcely notice it. We live under relentless pressure to perform well enough to reach that elusive "pot of gold." When it doesn't work out, we forever question ourselves. *I've been told all my life that it was possible, so I must be to blame.*

In his well-known book *Waking from the American Dream,* Donald McCullough describes how devastating this lie can be:

> We live in a culture that tells us our dreams can
> be realized with enough hard work and positive
> thinking. But, at one time or another, we wake up to
> reality. We learn, often with great pain, that we can't
> always have what we desperately want. Perhaps a
> marriage leaves us lonelier than we thought possible,
> or a single life feels like an inescapable prison, or sex-
> ual drives remain frustrated, or vocational advance-
> ment has been blocked, or health evades us, or God
> seems to have locked Himself in an unresponsive

heaven—disappointment comes in a variety of ways, and it can send us straight into the pit.[4]

The drive for success doesn't stop there. Even if we end up in the emotional pit, there remains the compelling belief that, despite our frustrations and disappointments, our salvation is still based on our ability to succeed and perform. We honestly believe that we must find some way, some outlet, some book or seminar that will grant us the ability to stand tall when everything and everyone around us is crumbling.

Current business wisdom tells us that the way to achieve success is to find something we're good at, because everybody excels at something. Surely, then, the path to satisfaction in life is not to "succeed," since that is an elusive goal. Rather, the idea goes, it is to find our own niche within which we can achieve our personalized version of success.

But what happens when we do perform up to our own limited expectations? Are we happy then? Fulfilled? Do we find freedom from the driving need to perform successfully? No, maintains Robert McGee, who claims that this philosophy of life is sorely lacking:

> A primary deception all of us tend to believe is that success will bring fulfillment and happiness. Again and again, we've tried to measure up, thinking that if we could meet certain standards, we would feel good about ourselves. But again and again, we've failed and have felt miserable. Even if we succeed on a fairly regular basis, occasional failure may be so devastating that it dominates our perception of ourselves.[5]

Finding my niche in life, and ultimately discovering at least a glimpse of the gifts and talents I possess, is a healthy way to reinforce a foundational belief in myself as a valuable person. But even the realization that I have something valuable to offer is not enough. As long as I believe that there is any possibility that I can make myself feel valuable by what I do, I remain hounded by the performance illusion. I am destined to live my life enslaved to a system that tells me I can make it only if I try harder.

To combat the forces around me that tell me I must *do* more in order to *be* more, my focus has to change. Instead of allowing "doing" goals to control me, I can set goals for my inward journey toward freedom in Christ to bring me to wholeness. Instead of looking to external success for fulfillment, in Christ I find the hope of a more powerful way to live than any I have ever known.

OUR CULTURE INSISTS THAT BUSYNESS IS OVER GODLINESS

Eugene Peterson once remarked that "busyness is laziness." He meant that it is far easier to be swept along by the current of the day — where there is never enough time to accomplish all that is "necessary" — than it is to stop, breathe deeply, and take control of our lives. In staying mindlessly busy, we act like automatons who have been programed to *react* to life, rather than people who are called to *live* life. Yes, busyness is laziness; yet it's more — it's destructive.

Who isn't too busy these days? Everyone I meet never seems to have enough time. We don't have enough time for friendships, for thinking, for dreaming. We don't have enough time to reflect on what really matters because we are too busy.

Dee and I have spent the last few years writing and speaking in the area of healthy families and marriages. One foundational principle we hold dear is the importance of quality *and* quantity time for families. Quality time says that I value you enough to make sure our time together is wisely spent; quantity time says that I enjoy you, and every moment I have with you is precious.

We recommend that couples start by committing to

each other for a one-on-one date at least every two weeks. So many couples tell us they don't have time for anything close to that: "Other things are more urgent — time with the kids (which is valuable), our work (which is necessary), our church (which is noble, or covertly expected, depending on our position and whom we are talking to at the time)." But what is more important than spending time with each other? There is an old saying, "Never sacrifice the important for the urgent." Kids' needs, work responsibilities, and church involvement — even for those in vocational ministry — are all very good ways to spend time, but *never* at the sacrifice of time as a couple.

Take this example to any area of your life, and you will see how reactive our lives have become. Unless you are an invalid or in prison, no one forces a schedule on you; you are busy because you have chosen to be busy. And so am I. I *want* to slow down, to stop, to "waste time" with those I love, to take walks or ride bikes without having to chalk up points in a fitness program. But I must fight my programing to "get busy!"

Every time I told somebody about this book, I got the same response. A friend called me and asked what I was doing. "Writing a book on the ethic of performance that we need to fight," I replied. "No kidding?" my friend exclaimed. "I want to be a case study — let me tell you what I'm struggling with. . . ." And on it went.

Everywhere I turn, I see busy people. Harried people. Insecure, lonely, fed-up, discouraged people who want to slow down, say no to the messages that are beating them down, and take a deep breath of freedom.

4

TRUST AND OBEY

When we walk with the Lord in the light of His Word,
What a glory He sheds on our way!
While we do His good will, He abides with us still,
And with all who will trust and obey.

Trust and obey, for there's no other way
To be happy in Jesus, but to trust and obey.

For we never can prove the delights of His love
Until all on the altar we lay.
For the favor He shows and the joy He bestows
Are for those who will trust and obey. So we'll . . .

Trust and obey, for there's no other way
To be happy in Jesus, but to trust and obey.

I remember the first time I heard this old gospel song. Even then, at sixteen years old and a relative newcomer to the world of personal faith, I had mixed feelings. Obviously, there is great biblical truth in the lyrics, and the tune is catchy, but something still rankles me today.

I think I know what it is: *Where is my faith when I stumble?* What about when I'm sitting on the side of the road resting my weary feet, and I see all those other "superstar Christians" apparently passing me by in their glowing walk with the Lord? What then? Do *I* get a "glory shed" on *my* way?

The second verse *really* frightens me, to be truly honest. "For we never can prove the delights of His love until all on the altar we lay. . . ." I *try* to do that—I think I *usually* do that. But when I look deep down inside, I know that I spend most of my life recognizing and admitting I still have a long way to go. Then the battle begins in earnest. I fall, I cry, I deny, I sit up, I stand, and I go on again—over and over again. Must I be reminded every time I sing this song that

I can *never* "prove the delights of His love"?

I guess I *am* in trouble . . . "For the favor He shows and the joy He bestows are for those who will trust and obey." I'm doomed to be deprived of experiencing either favor or joy from God because I don't always "trust and obey." Taking this song at face value, I can get depressed whenever I hear it.

I'm sure that most people who have grown up with this song have no problem whatsoever with its lyrics. I may even have offended some individuals by what I've said. But I take that risk believing that there are many people who *do* feel the way I do. They honestly want to trust and to obey. But in their attempts to live up to these ideals, they stumble over such personal and cleverly-disguised limitations and failures that secretly they feel as if they have no right even to sing such a song.

Where *do* our failures of faith leave us?

NOBODY'S PERFECT

At issue here is how we understand what it means, practically, to "trust and obey." The Apostle James provides some insights for us in his caution to teachers:

> Not many of you should presume to be teachers, my
> brothers, because you know that we who teach will
> be judged more strictly. We all stumble in many
> ways. If anyone is never at fault in what he says, he is
> a perfect man, able to keep his whole body in check.
> (James 3:1-2)

And who but Jesus is a "perfect man, able to keep his whole body in check"? James has already answered this question—"we all stumble in many ways." Teachers are not above failure, and therefore they must be willing to recognize their awesome responsibility and respond with great humility and proper caution.

So even those "superstar Christians" who pass me on the road as I sit resting my weary feet must struggle with shadows as they walk in the light of His Word. In this reminder James helps us debunk the myth of perfection in our response to the call to trust and obey.

The Apostle Paul also helps us gain a practical understanding of what it means to "trust and obey." Paul seemed to grow in his understanding of his own failures and limitations as the years molded and shaped him and his ministry. I first noticed this when I heard a tape some years ago entitled *Bearing and Sharing*, by Bruce Theilman, a Presbyterian minister. In the context of calling us to love and care for one another openly and honestly, Theilman identifies the following progression in the life and theology of Paul:

SEQUENCE OF PAUL'S DEEPENING WALK WITH CHRIST
A. In Paul's first letter (Galatians 1:1) he lays claim to the highest office: "Paul, an apostle. . . ."
B. Seven years later to the Corinthians he wrote: "Paul, least of the apostles and not worthy to be called an apostle."
C. Eight years after that he wrote to the Ephesians and said: "Unto me, less than the least of the saints, was grace given."
D. Finally, at the very end of his ministry he wrote to his young son in the faith, Timothy, "Christ Jesus came into the world to save sinners, of which I am chief."

As Paul deepened in his experience he opened himself more and more to both the beautiful and the ugly about himself.[1]

These statements, each of which is fully true, express a definite pattern of growth in Paul's understanding. Paul knew exactly who he was and where he stood in relation to where he *should* have been standing. He was well aware that he got angry, jealous, sometimes hurt others, and so on. But as he grew in his awareness of his failures, he also grew in his ability to admit his frailties freely and openly to others in the fellowship of believers.

This kind of searching vulnerability seems rare among believers today. Instead, we are burdened by a theology of performance. Simply put, it teaches that our obedience is what "unleashes" God's power in our lives and allows us to experience His love. I believe that this is a distortion of biblical truth and an affront to the gospel. Rather, our performance (or obedience) in relationship to God is a *result* of our experience of His love and our understanding of who we are in Christ (we will explore this further in part 2). This is what Paul communicates in Galatians 2:20-21:

> I have been crucified with Christ and I no longer live, but Christ lives in me. The life I live in the body, I live by faith in the Son of God, who loved me and gave himself for me. I do not set aside the grace of God, for if righteousness could be gained through the law [of performance], Christ died for nothing!

In creating the expectation that we must achieve certain obedience standards to be happy and fulfilled in our walk with the Lord, the "Christian culture" of our day has created another version of the performance treadmill. Let's look at some components of this theology of performance: church attendance, prayer, and Bible study.

CHURCH ATTENDANCE AS DEVOTIONAL DUTY

Growing up, the only exposure I had to Catholics were the few kids I went to school with. We rarely talked about matters of faith, but I remember being told that the difference between "us" and Catholics was "*they* have to go to church *every* Sunday," even though my family attended our church on a regular basis. The difference was in the "have to." In the churches I grew up in, attendance was important but optional. That was before I personally met Christ.

In my early days as a sincere and committed follower of Christ, the churches I attended didn't have a Pope or church councils to define for us what was or wasn't expected. However, that didn't mean that there weren't clear and definite expectations.

Take church attendance, for example. No one ever actually *told* me that I must go to church three times a week—Sunday morning, Sunday evening, and Wednesday night—but I somehow knew that if I was "really serious" about my faith, this attendance pattern was not optional. Notice that phrase, "really serious." This was often how the expectations around me were labeled. If I decided to miss a Sunday for, say, a Forty-Niners football game, then I wasn't "really serious" about my faith, and therefore I wasn't a "really serious Christian." It's not much of a jump to see how my perception was formed of how God felt about someone missing church.

Going to church—and more than that, being *involved* in a local body—is good, valuable, and important for growth in Christ. Being a follower of Christ is not a solo adventure, it is a call to community—to know one another, and as much as possible to live in connection to others who share the same faith. But once the coming together is relegated to a "have to," it loses its meaning for spiritual growth.

Biblically, church attendance is actually community involvement. The weekly assembly, then, is a coming together of believers to be mutually encouraged, to be taught, and to be sent out for ministry. But for many today, it is simply an hour of devotional duty. Most contemporary churches call their weekly meeting a "worship service," but in reality it is actually the single point of contact between the institution and its members. Even when a church has decided to forego making the service do and be everything for the community, biblical worship is still just one part of the local church's reason for being.

Recently, some friends of mine who had been believers

for decades were delighting in the fact that their church had "finally done away with the Sunday evening service." One went on to exclaim, "Now we can finally have one night for our family, instead of having to go to church." This person was not a new convert to the faith. She is a leader in the Christian community of her city. Her stated opinion simply reflected how the current Christian culture has taken what is good and made it another way to perform for God and others. We go to church because we're *supposed* to go.

WHEN PRAYER DOESN'T "WORK"

Prayer is a seldom practiced but often discussed exercise. For many, it is a constant source of frustration. Despite the flood of books, teaching, and discussion, it remains perhaps the most difficult aspect of the believer's life.

One reason for this difficulty involves our expectations about prayer. "Prayer changes things," proclaims the overused expression. Why, then, doesn't prayer *always* change things? Maybe it's because we don't pray enough. Then why should we keep at it if nothing ever happens when we *do* pray?

One writer put the difficulty this way:

> Most of us don't pray as much as we feel we should, not because we are unwilling, but because we are uncertain how to pray and don't understand why our prayers aren't answered more consistently. It is frustrating to keep doing something that you are not sure is working.[2]

James adds to this confusion:

> Is any one of you in trouble? He should pray. Is anyone happy? Let him sing songs of praise. Is any one of you sick? He should call the elders of the church to pray over him and anoint him with oil in the name

of the Lord. And the prayer offered in faith will make the sick person well; the Lord will raise him up. If he has sinned, he will be forgiven. Therefore confess your sins to each other and pray for each other so that you may be healed. The prayer of a righteous man is powerful and effective. (James 5:13-16)

Burned into my memory is an experience involving a friend who was going through a painful time in his life. His father was gravely ill, his job situation was especially difficult, and he was feeling as though the Lord had left him. My friend had taken the risk of sharing all this in a small group of ministry acquaintances. One member of the group, an energetic, loud, and often brash older woman, had seen his sharing as an opportunity for a "teachable moment." She opened to this passage in James (5:13-16) and began to tell my friend that the problems in his life were due to "unconfessed sin" and a lack of "righteous" prayer. She was all ready to "fix" him, when my friend suddenly bolted out of the room, and ultimately out of this particular ministry and away from this group of people . . . for good.

Biblical prayer is a complex, seemingly contradictory mass of disjointed information that can never be definitively understood. There are some things we do know from the scriptural record: God will respond to prayer, sometimes in the way we ask Him to; God does want us to pray, and often; in the Lord's prayer Jesus gave us an idea of the kind of prayer content that pleases God, but it is not the only model for prayer; God wants to give us what we ask for; and God seems to allow and even encourage us to pester Him in our prayers.

These are what we know for sure about prayer. But sometimes in our efforts to fill in the gaps of what we *don't* know, is it possible that we go so far as to make *ourselves* the focus of prayer?

When my friend poured out his heart that night, was he in need of a neat, clean formula that would deliver him from his problems and pain? Or was he in need of something far deeper—a source of comfort that would not necessarily "fix" him but could bring him through his trials? This woman, in her sincere desire to help, caused him to feel more pain when he left than when he arrived. In effect, she attempted to persuade him that he was responsible for his state of suffering—and perhaps even the source of his own salvation. "If you would only pray, *then.* . . ." The message of the performance ethic was clear: God is immovable and unresponsive unless you jump through a series of predetermined hoops. And if that doesn't work? You must not be praying the "prayer of a righteous man."

But that is far from the whole story when it comes to prayer. The Bible clearly indicates that God is not so much interested in *relieving* our suffering as He is intent on having our suffering *draw us to Him.* He understands suffering more than any of us could, for the agony that Jesus endured both physically and spiritually goes far beyond any possible human experience. We may be tempted to seek instant assistance from God for banishing all suffering from our lives, but God knows better. His gift to us is His identification with us and compassion for us through our trials and pain. "Because he himself suffered when he was tempted, he is able to help those who are being tempted" (Hebrews 2:18).

Pain, hardship, and suffering are with us as long as we live in this world. But the proponents of performance theology have reduced the Bible to a simplistic legal contract between the believer and God, in which prayer is a simple transaction that triggers God's response in changing things. This view leaves very little room for acknowledging the reality of this world. And it places us on a dangerous treadmill, because we then hold ourselves responsible for whether or not God answers our prayer. As a result, when it comes time to suffer, cry, hurt, and wonder, "Why, God, why?" there will be no answers. The heavens will seem void, and our despair plunges deeper.

However we look at prayer, we can be sure about the

constancy of God's heart behind all the gaps and riddles and unanswered questions of prayer. Although the compassionate nature of God's heart is plainly presented throughout Scripture, it is especially obvious in 2 Corinthians 1:3-5, where the Apostle Paul speaks of his own suffering. Perhaps this is one of the best places to step off the performance treadmill in our understanding of prayer:

> Praise be to the God and Father of our Lord Jesus Christ, the Father of compassion and the God of all comfort, who comforts us in all our troubles, so that we can comfort those in any trouble with the comfort we ourselves have received from God. For just as the sufferings of Christ flow over into our lives, so also through Christ our comfort overflows.

WHEN BIBLE STUDY IS REDUCED
TO A RELIGIOUS REQUIREMENT

Most of my adult life I have been involved in working with youth and leadership training of youth ministers. One of the most common statements that youth leaders make to encourage young people to pursue their faith is, "It is important for you to have a daily quiet time."

The concept of the quiet time ranks high among Christian cultural duties. Again, as in expectations of church attendance and prayer, it is not so much a verbalized requirement as an unwritten rule of modern evangelical faith.

It's interesting that when this statement is made, it's usually presented in a casual and offhand way—with the implication that *of course* you must have a daily quiet time to be a vital believer! After all, Jesus arose early each morning to pray—the argument states—so every believer must do this regularly, too. In my experience, however, the vast majority of the leaders who present such a message are rarely if ever able to practice the discipline of a daily quiet time consistently. We tell kids one thing and we rationalize another.

And I'm afraid this is not limited to those in youth ministry.

There are, of course, many sincere and devout believers who *are* able to discipline their lives in such a way that daily devotions are a regular event. For these individuals, this practice usually deepens their experience of Christ significantly. But, on the other hand, simply having a daily quiet time is by no means a guarantee of a healthy and vibrant faith relationship free from the need to perform. In fact the reverse is often true, for the greatest danger of highly structured people is to place that same level of expectation on others, thus proving only that they themselves are caught up in the ethic of performance.

Reading the Bible, praying, and getting involved in a church body are all important and valuable tools in helping us to exercise our love for Christ. The tendency with any spiritual discipline, however, is to order it and systematize it as a way to ensure that it becomes a regular practice in the life of every believer. As noble and helpful as this sounds, it contains a serious drawback—it can reduce faith to a mere religion, with rules and expectations, which becomes our attempt to please a distant and uninterested God.

But we don't need to engage in religious practices to get God's attention. The God of the Bible is anything but distant, for the Incarnation proves that God understands and actively participates in the everyday affairs of His people. And neither is God uninterested, for the entire Bible from Genesis to Revelation sounds His passionate pleas for His children to return to the love relationship He desires with each one.

Religion has been defined as "people's attempt to get to God," in contrast to faith as God's attempt to reach people. We must learn how to listen to that Voice who is ever calling, ever seeking. To us it may be a whisper, but in heaven it resounds with thunder! Those who obscure the sound of His majestic offer of peace by adding rules and placing burdens on His children must "Wake up, O sleeper, and rise from the dead!"

5

THE "BLAMING" SYNDROME—"IT'S NOT MY FAULT!"

L isa didn't want to talk, especially to me. She wasn't mad, exactly, she just wasn't in the mood. But the question I asked her changed all that.

Lisa was an attractive, popular junior involved in our Young Life club. Because of the time Dee had spent with her, she had become fairly close to our kids and Dee. At our meetings she listened intently to me when I spoke about Jesus Christ, and she seemed to like me well enough. But whenever we were in a room together with just a few people she seemed to hold me at arm's length.

The summer following her junior year we were at a camp together and I had bet her a milk shake in some silly competition. She had accepted, but now as we sat alone on the porch of the Sugar Barrel, she wouldn't lift her eyes. I played a hunch I had carried for some time.

"Lisa, you don't have to answer this if you don't want to, but I'd like to ask you a question," I said.

"Okay."

"We have known you for a year now. You come over a lot and you are almost a part of our family; the kids love you! But something seems to be wrong between us. Lisa, do you struggle with me?"

Her eyes flashed up at me. "Why did you ask that?"

"I don't know, really. It's just that sometimes at home you'll be laughing and playing with everyone, but when I walk in you have to leave. I've also noticed that you will rarely look me in the eye. If I've done something to offend you. . . ."

"It's not you," she murmured, "it's me. . . ."

Silence as we both looked away. Then she began to talk. Slowly at first, but as her story began to unfold she became more deliberate. As we reached the second hour, I knew that this was a sacred moment, and she would never be the same.

When Lisa was five years old, the son of a daycare worker had molested her. For years she had kept silent, hoarding her secret, wondering why this had happened to her. Without even realizing it, Lisa began to shut out men, beginning with her father. She had told only one friend, but that friend hadn't said much. Now, as Lisa talked, she began the long trek to recovery.

When we got home, Lisa told her parents what had happened. Within the next few days I met with her and her father, and they soon found a counselor they both trusted who helped them work through years of pain. Today Lisa is engaged to be married, a college graduate with a vibrant faith. She is deeply involved working with junior high students, and she enjoys a wonderfully healed relationship with her father. From all indications, her counseling has been a resounding success. She was one of the lucky ones.

Lisa opened up on her own, and she responded well to the counseling process. Now, five years later, Lisa's scars of pain have become beauty marks that God has used to touch others. But the process was long and difficult. Her pain was real.

TRAUMA IN WESTERN CULTURE

Lisa's story is not unique, not by a long shot. Abuse, abandonment, the pain of divorce, severe family problems — these are but a sampling of the sources of anguish underlying the surface of Western — especially American — culture.

Others struggle with a deep-seated insecurity and feel the need for help even though they have not experienced such obviously traumatic events. I can't recall a significant incident (or person) that has harmed me, yet I often struggle with guilt, frustration, and the fear of not "measuring up."

Whatever the causes of these internal struggles, people in our society are attending therapy groups, self-help groups, and counseling sessions in record numbers. This sharp increase in attention to what has become known as family dysfunction has taken the counseling world by storm. But not everyone is pleased with the direction this movement has been taking.

CURRENT CRITIQUES
OF THE RECOVERY MOVEMENT

A newspaper article entitled "Dysfunction Junction" appeared last year that criticized John Bradshaw, a well-known author and workshop leader in the area of family dysfunction, for encouraging his patients to place blame on their parents. In Bradshaw's best-selling book *Homecoming*, he quotes a woman in her seventies who was instructed to write a letter to her deceased mother to "express" her anger in the attempt to be helped:

> Mother, you were too busy with your charity work. You never had time to tell me you loved me. You paid attention to me only when I was sick or when I was playing the piano and making *you* proud. You only

let me have the feelings that pleased you. You never loved me for myself.

"Bradshaw," wrote Tim Larimer, author of the article, "is quick to point out, 'Remember, I am not blaming any-one's parents. They were wounded adult children trying to do an enormously difficult task.'"

Larimer continues, "Oh, kind of like: *Happy Mother's Day. I know you tried.*"[1]

The article is aimed at providing a balancing perspective on the "recovery movement" that is affecting large segments of the American adult population. Larimer describes the phenomenon of blaming parents as a natural human impulse that is part of our culture. Although he concedes that the various recovery and therapy groups are meeting real needs, he points out that many people have "jumped on the bandwagon of blame" and are lashing out. He quotes one therapist who is similarly disenchanted with this dimension of the recovery movement:

> I've been to a fair number of twelve-step groups, and they remind me of being 15 years old sometimes. I'm talking about the kind of complaining and whining that goes on. It's OK when you're 15 or 16 years old, but when people are doing that at 35 and 45, the whole nation is in a state of arrested development.[2]

The article fascinated me. But I felt that the author was tossing off a simplistic "grow up and cope" to those on the fringes of severe loneliness, frustration, and pain. In essence, he said that it was time for America to get off the blaming kick, abolish the word "dysfunction" from our vocabulary, and take some responsibility. He did not, however, offer any alternatives, and neither did his sources—therapists, lecturers, and authors.

This critique of the recovery movement is echoed in other segments of the professional community as well. As

Larimer recounts, "Therapist Stephen Wolin recently told a crowd of four thousand colleagues: 'I believe the recovery movement, and its lopsided counsel of damage, has become dangerous.' The crowd leapt to its feet and gave Wolin a standing ovation."[3] Larimer also quotes Ted Turner's therapist, Frank Pittman, as saying, "A society full of victims is a bunch of people who have a free pass not to take responsibility for their actions."[4]

These perspectives make me wonder if some in the counseling world are simply sick and tired of the cries of despair from the clients they deal with daily, even though the majority may be in real need of help.

CAUSES BEHIND THE RECOVERY MOVEMENT

To be concerned, alarmed, or even frightened by the current wave of recovery groups is understandable considering the popularity of the "family dysfunction" concept and the proliferation of the victim mentality. What these learned men and women fail to mention in their critiques, however, is the *cause* of such a movement. To write off the entire movement as mere childishness or even an unwillingness to take responsibility is sheer arrogance.

Our culture faces very real problems, and people are legitimately seeking relief. Yes, there are recovery groups for such seemingly lightweight addictions as shopping, sleeping, and even jogging. There are even groups for people who have been abused and beaten down by what they would call "dysfunctional" churches. But there is nothing superficial about these struggles for those who suffer through them. The deeper question is this: *What is the source of this enormous cry for help and understanding?* Is it simply the narcissistic indulgence of a pampered and selfish generation, who have nothing better to do than sit around and complain about how badly they have been mistreated?

We have looked at several areas of our lives in which we have been barraged with the performance ethic. In any one of these areas taken alone, these messages might have the power to convince us that we are unlovely and unworthy apart from how we perform. But when all of these messages are piled one on top of another, the mound of guilt and frustration can form an eclipse that blocks out any ray of hope.

ASSIGNING BLAME IS NOT THE ANSWER

It can be argued that *many* of the problems we face—guilt, loneliness, a gnawing sense of frustration—may indeed have been spawned by people or circumstances in our lives. However, to blame our stress and anxiety on others, on specific circumstances, or even on God is not the path to freedom. Blaming only drives us deeper into a world where we are ultimately alone, seeking retribution for the pain we feel, but neither satisfied nor any closer to healing.

Behind the blaming is fear, thinly shrouded in a subtle and arrogant determination to get my own way. If I believe that you will not like me when you see how deep my problems are, I will try to appear untouchable. Or if I believe that I have to perform for you, I will flee, because I can't take any more messages pointing out how miserably I'm failing. I will not give you the chance to hurt me more than I have been hurt already. I will keep you at arm's length. Blaming can be a way of doing that.

This is where the church can provide incredible healing and support, but it is also the place where the church can be even more destructive if it promotes the performance ethic in our faith. This is when our impulse to hide or to flee is most damaging. When we hear a message reminding us of how far we are from where God requires us to be, we can no longer trust our struggles to God or His representatives.

Have you ever been wounded by the church? There are countless people in our culture who harbor an inner longing for God but who have rejected the Christian institution. Usually they blame the church for some negative incident, such as an oppressive Sunday school teacher, or a personality conflict with others in the church, or sometimes a devastating breach of trust, as when a member of the clergy falls. Some go even further and blame God for their problems with the church, responding to hurt by rationalizing away their faith.

Have you turned to blame in order to assuage the hurt in your soul? As natural as it may feel, blaming is not the answer to your pain, frustration, or brokenness. Your first step in releasing the hold of the performance illusion is to recognize the source of your pain. The best way to do that is to let go of the false notion that you are alone. Counseling and group recovery programs *can* be helpful in providing insight and support. For just about all of us, there comes a time when we get so confused and frustrated by our behaviors, feelings, and responses that we need to seek some help in the form of counseling.

THE ROLE OF COUNSELING

Counseling from a Christian perspective is a great gift in its potential for offering biblical guidance, facilitating self-discovery, and providing an atmosphere in which healing can take place. But at its best, counseling can only help us to understand life, especially our own, more clearly. In and of itself, counseling cannot heal.

The counselor's task, then, is to help clients explore the hidden nooks and crannies of their minds and emotions as seen from a Kingdom of God perspective. The goal is to help counselees understand why they act (or react) in a particular way, what factors have contributed to those behaviors, and how God loves them freely, without conditions. The next task is to provide skills that will enable them to move on, no longer shackled by hidden messages and spontaneous, uncontrollable responses.

Once the clients have gained an understanding of their behavior(s) and acquired skills to deal with them, they need a group of friends who are willing to stand alongside them, helping in the pursuit of health. The counselor's job is finished, at least for a season, for it is now the responsibility of the individual and the helping community to act on what they know.

Many people are more comfortable ignoring their struggles than admitting they have a problem. Others find it easier to try to shut out the messages of defeat from performance promoters than to find a counselor they can trust. But if what they feel is more than a fleeting bout with depression, sooner or later the struggle will surface and they will be forced to face it.

Just as blaming others can be a way of ignoring our struggles, going it alone—or even trying to "buck up"—can also be a form of hiding. That doesn't mean it is necessarily bad to "tough it out," especially if only for a season. However, our ability to abandon the performance illusion and get on with the healing process is ultimately dependent on *where* we hide.

THE GIFT OF HIDING

Deep down I believe that no one honestly wishes to hide in personal pain and suffering. But sometimes we may be so wounded that we have no choice. In childhood it may be a necessary means of self-protection, or even for a period of time immediately following a traumatic crisis. But the longer we hide our feelings—from others, ourselves, or even God—the greater our need becomes to find a place of refuge where we can be honest with our struggles.

Obviously, we need to be careful and selective about where we reveal this most fragile side of our lives. In this fallen world, indiscreet or open disclosure can come back to haunt us for years. But in order for healing to take place, the one place we *must* go with complete vulnerability is into the arms of the One who created us.

The psalmist provides a picture of what occurs on the inside when we hide our struggles from the Lord:

When I kept silent,
>   my bones wasted away
>   through my groaning all day long.
For day and night
>   your hand was heavy upon me;
my strength was sapped
>   as in the heat of summer. (Psalm 32:3-4)

What amazing honesty from the one who was so loved by God! And yet David doesn't leave us there. As the psalm continues we see what happens when we stop hiding from God and reveal our hearts to Him with complete honesty and openness:

Then I acknowledged my sin to you
>   and did not cover up my iniquity.
I said, "I will confess
>   my transgressions to the Lord" –
and you forgave
>   the guilt of my sin.
Therefore let everyone who is godly pray to you
>   while you may be found;
surely when the mighty waters rise,
>   they will not reach him.
You are my hiding place;
>   you will protect me from trouble
>   and surround me with songs of deliverance.
>   (Psalm 32:5-7)

When we hide in the safety and tenderness of our "gracious and compassionate" God, we are empowered to be honest with ourselves, and ultimately to find a group of friends with whom we can freely and openly share the deepest parts of our lives. This is an empowerment for healing, for when we hide in our Lord we discover that the healing of our hearts is what matters most to Him.

6

"I Did It My Way": The Deity of Loneliness

A few years ago I was asked to speak at a Christian rock festival in Kentucky called ICTHUS. Yes, it was as fun as it sounds—three days of rain, blaring rock, fifteen thousand young people, and four porta-potties. What a blast! Anyway, I was there to speak on dating, relationships, and sexuality, in connection with a book and video series I had done entitled *Next Time I Fall in Love*. During my presentation I mentioned how a solid friendship is at the core of any healthy dating relationship.

On Saturday night a young woman approached me at the book table, where I was packing up the unsold copies of *Next Time*. She asked to buy a book, and then queried me about my insistence on friendship as part of a dating relationship. After five minutes of light and almost silly discussion she asked for my address, and smiling, she left. I didn't think much about her after that.

On the following Wednesday I received an unusual letter. Up in the left-hand corner of the envelope there was written in tiny letters, "Nobody." I had never received a letter from Nobody before. Here's what she said:

> Dear Chap,
>   Hi. What's up? Not much here! I want to explain why I questioned you about the word friend. I don't like (hate) myself so I figure I have no friends. I hate the word friend. I figure it's okay to say this to you because I sorta trust you. I hate myself so I figure you ought to also. I dunno why I got your book, maybe I got it to prepare myself if some guy ever shows any interest in me. I'm 20 years old and no guy has ever looked at me, asked me out, or shown any interest in me. I guess I really am ugly. (Yeah, I even hate my eyes.) I gotta go, I told you too much already. Sorry I took so much time, good bye.
>
>   Mary
>
> P.S. Don't laugh when you read this letter. OK???[1]

I didn't laugh. I'm not the kind of guy who cries easily (at least, I wasn't until I started dealing with my own sense of loneliness a couple of years ago), but I wept for Mary. My tears began with a sadness for her, and I felt incredulous at her ability to articulate her pain so clearly. But soon my tears changed focus—I wept for myself out of guilt. I am a youth minister—my whole adult life has been dedicated to listening to kids, loving kids, helping kids; and in my busyness I missed her. I was overcome by my inability to realize in that brief encounter that she was crying out for someone who would break through her facade of giddiness. I could have let her know that I understood, and that I cared. But I missed her.

But then something else happened inside me. As I continued to cry, I realized that I was no longer thinking about Mary. I was thinking about me! As often as I'd gone through the motions of being a "professional" minister, I'd had many days when *I* could have written that letter. What Mary had so eloquently stated, I have felt. I sometimes experience dark days of loneliness and depressing intro-spection. I sometimes wonder if anyone likes me for who I am instead of what I do. Although I know better, I even sometimes secretly question Dee's love for me: "Would she still love me if I lost my job, or missed a few mortgage payments?"

I realized that Mary and I were cut from the same cloth: the fabric of loneliness, isolation, and fear. The only difference was that she had not learned how to fill her life so full of the insignificant that she was able to blot out the despair in her heart. I am better at it than she, and when I recognized that, I knew I was in far more trouble. My walls are thicker—and therefore more potent, impregnable, and battle-hardened.

Although I knew I had lived Mary's letter, I don't think I could have admitted it, even to myself, until that day. Most of my life I have sought approval and recognition based on my performance, which in turn has caused me to live behind a wall of apparent self-confidence. But the harder I tried to fit in and look good, the harder it has been for me to be myself. It was like playing different roles at different times, and it would get to the point where sometimes I couldn't tell where the role ended and the real me began. During those times I felt more like an actor on stage than a feeling, thinking, responding person.

In that state it was hard for me to reach out to anyone else, and I made it hard for anyone to reach out to me. The more I tried to perform by living up to someone else's idea of who I was supposed to be, the more I internally distanced myself from the very ones who could help free me from the *need* to perform—my friends, my wife, my children, even my God.

When I shared my revelation from Mary's letter with a friend, a successful advertising executive, he remarked, "I believe that the loneliest people in our culture are men, especially successful men. They spend so many of their early adult years building and selling and fighting and running that they have little time and energy for anything else. Then, as they near age forty and beyond, there finally arrives the time to stop and think. That's when they suddenly realize how alone they are." The performance illusion may have brought them more success, but the quickening pace also brought them a more complicated and demanding life.

Ironically, the more people try to achieve peace, happiness, and security by making their mark in business or in their occupation, the greater their disappointment and disillusionment. Freedom from the performance treadmill never comes by living up to its demands. The first step of freedom is recognizing how the drive to perform cuts us off from those we need most.

In *The Friendless American Male,* David W. Smith made this observation:

> For most of us, our problem is not with our jobs but rather with ourselves. It is not our job that contributes to the calamity of our friendless condition or our psychosomatic disorders, but rather how we view ourselves, and how we think and behave, that get us into trouble. We have learned to withstand and keep to ourselves pain, loneliness, fear and anything else that has a taint of humanness. Indeed we believe that we have to withstand feelings, and have been so taught. . . . Someone once wrote that the birthright of the American male is a chronic sense of personal inadequacy (and that) the American masculine dream is killing us.[2]

Due to the persuasiveness of the performance ethic in our world, loneliness is our greatest cultural cancer.

Mary is lonely, but not alone. She is just more honest than most. But there is more to our loneliness that is often

missed. Loneliness can be a gift, as Henri Nouwen counsels us:

> Therefore I would like to voice loudly and clearly
> what might seem unpopular and maybe even disturb-
> ing: The Christian way of life does not take away our
> loneliness; it protects and cherishes it as a precious
> gift. Sometimes it seems as if we do everything pos-
> sible to avoid the painful confrontation with our basic
> human loneliness, and allow ourselves to be trapped
> by false gods promising immediate satisfaction and
> quick relief.
>
> But perhaps the painful awareness of loneliness
> is an invitation to transcend our limitations and
> look beyond the boundaries of our existence. The
> awareness of loneliness reveals to us an inner emp-
> tiness that can be destructive when misunderstood,
> but filled with promise for those who can tolerate its
> sweet pain.[3]

In chapter 5 I spoke of the privilege and the need we
all have of hiding in the arms of God. So many sincere and
devout believers seem to worry constantly about the quality of their faith and the depth of their commitment simply because they still struggle with the performance ethic—
especially in the face of loneliness. As I counsel students at
our seminary, I often discover a deep, gnawing sense of guilt
over an emptiness and loneliness that no amount of faith can
take away.

The problem, however, is not in the Christian commitment of these men and women. The problem is in the false
packaging we have received about what the life of faith is
all about.

To follow Christ doesn't mean we will be delivered from
the struggles and problems that all sinful people face. In
fact, when we commit our lives to following Jesus Christ
we are accepting a much more difficult, and at times more

painful, road. I read that C. S. Lewis once commented, "I didn't become a Christian to be happy; a pint of port will work far better."

Even for the most devout, loneliness will always be present. But it can be a gift—as a reminder of our constant need for companionship with God. In Christ, we have the ability to choose whether to sink down in despair or reach out to "the Father of compassion and the God of all comfort, who comforts us in all our troubles" (2 Corinthians 1:3-4).

Jesus said, "If anyone would come after me, he must deny himself and take up his cross daily and follow me. For whoever wants to save his life will lose it, but whoever loses his life for me will save it" (Luke 9:23-24). His invitation is radical, but it is also straightforward. To follow Jesus means to come to Him with all that we are and all that we carry—including the burden of our loneliness, our pain, and our need to perform.

7

WHAT'S GONE WRONG?

An extremely frightening characteristic of our culture today is secrecy. We have learned how to keep quiet about who we are and what's going on inside of us. We're afraid to share our innermost thoughts with anyone. As a result, we see and know each other largely from the outside, with only glimpses of who we really are. It's just easier and safer to hide. Most of our energy goes into keeping up a good front—all the while painfully aware of how broken we are on the inside.

Why do we have such a need to prove ourselves? What is the root cause of the dominance of the performance ethic? Why do others try to control us with their own agendas and expectations, and why do we seek such power for ourselves? Why do all of us feel so lonely and inadequate, and yet so few of us have the courage to admit it? And, ultimately, if there is a God who cares, why has He allowed us to be so enslaved to our needs for perfection, conformity, and success? What on earth has gone wrong?

Everything. There is a war being waged every day in every part of the planet. Its casualties are astronomical and global in scope. This conflict is hardly ever discussed, however, and it is rarely taken seriously. The battle is not for territory or ideology; it is for power. And it is to the death.

The war is between two kingdoms: the kingdom of self and the Kingdom where Jesus Christ reigns as Lord. Every man, woman, and child who has ever lived resides at the heart of this battlefield. The struggle influences our every thought, motive, action, attitude, and conviction.

Understanding this conflict is the key to rejecting the performance illusion and learning to walk in freedom. Because of Jesus, all things have been given to us, but even the sincere believer must come to grips with the powers that seek to keep us from experiencing the life God has promised to us.

THE KINGDOM OF GOD
VERSUS THE KINGDOM OF SELF

In the beginning God had a beautiful plan. With unrestrained passion and infinite wisdom the Creator decided to make a world—not a jumbled mass of stone, water, and flesh, but a complex, intricate, and interdependent universe marked with the stamp of perfection. The Bible weaves a tapestry of intimacy in the Creation. Each atom was pieced together as tenderly as a child might cradle her kitten. Every animal had a reason, every tree a role to play, in this grand drama. And at the top, standing tall over the incredible and boundless majesty of the gift of Creation, is the crown, the greatest accomplishment of all, made in the very image of Perfect Love. *You.*

"No!" you protest. "We should all be there; we are all in this together. The whole human race stands together as one before God. Some days, I don't even feel I belong up there!"

For most people who believe that God is in the creation

business, there is no denying an element of truth in the fact that we all stand together as the pinnacle of creation. My theology, however, refuses to believe that God could be so intricate and specific in designing an individual snowflake, and yet reduce what the Bible calls the "crowning glory" to a mass assembly line.

Could God care about differences in fingerprints and yet make no relational distinctions in how He views people?

Couldn't be. God is not trivial. You are not just "one of many." You are absolutely and completely unique. God knew exactly what He was doing when He created you, and He is pleased with His work.

Occasionally I refer to my three offspring (one daughter, two sons) as "my kids" or "our children." I may even call them as a group—as in "Let's go, you guys. Get in the car!" But it is fundamentally impossible for me to relate to or even consider my children as a unit. Although they share the same "gene pool" and have many similarities, they are nothing alike; each is unique. If you ask me my about my family, I will describe them one by one, detailing the individual reasons why I am crazy about these three gifts the Lord has given Dee and me. I can't say, "My kids do this . . ." or "My kids are like that . . ." without quickly pointing out their distinctive, individual traits.

You are that distinctive and more. You were created as a beautiful and unblemished masterpiece of the Living God. You are one of many in the family of humanity, but you are also God's special person, created to live with Him for all eternity in intimate relationship.

This is God's plan. All of life has been created as a grand adventure for you within the context of your uniqueness and intimacy with the Father. Every flower, every relationship, every experience is a gift to be enjoyed and lived to the fullest. The beauty of this plan is that you have the privilege to live this life because God is right there with you, enabling you to live in the freedom of knowing that He is active in His care for you.

But God's beautiful plan allows for human choice. And so along came the Fall, when the creature decided to reject the Kingdom of the Creator and inaugurate the kingdom of self.

At first this human kingdom seemed so right, so natural. There was no law, no requisite for the one who resided on the throne here. As good as the Kingdom of God promised to be, the creature decided that it wasn't fair that God should reign, and so the creature made the deadly choice to leave the Kingdom of God and homestead on its own.

"How could God know what is best for me?" we have all asked as we have walked boldly away from the Kingdom of God. "I'm the best judge of *what* I want and *when* I want it!"

What's the cost of leaving the Kingdom of God, and what does that have to do with the ethic of performance that has enslaved us all?

When Jesus reigns as King, there is peace, and joy, and free celebration. When I reign as king, there is strife, fear, and darkness. How can I be at peace in a world where I am alone, vying for self-centered attention? How can I know joy, not just the padded cell of materialistic comfort and the temporary solace of side-tracking folly, when I live as a tourist from moment to moment, lusting for that next thrill or diversion that allows me to remain numb? Do I have any idea, as I wallow in the loneliness of the kingdom of self, what it means to celebrate life and love and freedom with others?

In God's Kingdom there is no need to perform to please anyone, for all members of the Kingdom know how infinitely pleasing they are, just as they are. In my kingdom, every ounce of energy, every moment of work or play, is consumed by my need to be taken seriously. I scream with all that I am, "Please, somebody, watch me! Look at me! Notice me! Love me!" So I perform, and I hope—and even sometimes pray—that somebody will take notice of me as I sit on my throne . . . proud, frightened, and hopelessly lonely.

Maybe at this point you are tiring of all this talk of two kingdoms: "I am a Christian; of *course* I live in the Kingdom of God!" And yet here is perhaps the most crucial issue in the struggle to abandon the performance illusion: your commitment to follow Christ doesn't mean that you are no longer influenced by the kingdom of self in your attitudes, values, behavior, or belief system.

When I acknowledged the inadequacy of life without Christ as Lord, I made the decision to hand over the deed to my life to God, and I was made new. But I still carried over into my new life the same patterns of behavior and ways of thinking I had relied on in my old life. As Paul says, I need to be taught how to put off the old self and learn how to be made new in the attitudes of my mind (Ephesians 4:22-23).

Learning to live "in Christ," then, means learning to "put off the old self." I am still learning how this affects my need to perform. Because of Jesus' great love for me, I am freed from the *need* to perform—but for most of my Christian life I simply didn't know that. When I *did* hear messages about freedom in Christ, there always seemed to be strings attached that reminded me this message wasn't quite true: "Yes, God loves you as you are—but if you *really* want to please Him, start earning those crowns!" (This is distinctly *not* a biblical concept, by the way—but I sure bought it!)

You may be a sincere follower of Christ who is actively seeking the Kingdom of God, but it's important for you to know that the performance illusion is sin seeking to have its way with you. As much as you may try to resist it, the seductive power of the kingdom of self is constantly urging you to trust yourself for all you need in life. The influence it continues to exert on you is what keeps you running on the performance treadmill.

Jesus' call to you is to look Him square in the eye, trust Him with your need to look good, do well, and be noticed, and stop running. The answer does not lie in doing more to please Him, for you are already as pleasing to Him as you can possibly be.

Notice the look in His eye. See His hand outstretched. Reach out. Grab it, as tightly as you can. Okay, now . . . jump!

PART TWO

What Must I Do to Be Saved?

▬

As for you, you were dead in your transgressions and
sins. . . . But because of his great love for us,
God, who is rich in mercy,
made us alive with Christ even when we were dead
in transgressions – it is by grace you have been saved.
And God raised us up with Christ and seated us with him
in the heavenly realms in Christ Jesus,
in order that in the coming ages he might show
the incomparable riches of his grace,
expressed in his kindness to us in Christ Jesus.
For it is by grace you have been saved, through faith –
and this not from yourselves, it is the gift of God –
not by works, so that no one can boast.
For we are God's workmanship,
created in Christ Jesus to do good works,
which God prepared in advance for us to do.

EPHESIANS 2:1,4-10

▬

In the evening I went very unwillingly to a society
in Aldersgate-Street, where one was reading Luther's
preface to the Epistle to the Romans.
About a quarter before nine, while he was describing
the change which God works in the heart through faith
in Christ, I felt my heart strangely warmed.
I felt I did trust in Christ, Christ alone for salvation:
And an assurance was given me, that he had taken away
my sins, even mine, and saved me
from the law of sin and death.

JOHN WESLEY

▬

Dear God
I don't ever feel alone since I found out about You.

NORA

77

8

Amazing Grace

For me, the highlight of the 1992 Summer Olympic games was watching runner Derek Redmond, a medalist hopeful for Great Britain. He reached the semifinals of the men's 400-meter race, but he never qualified for the finals. In fact, technically he didn't even finish the semifinal: "Race Abandoned" was the official designation. But anyone who saw his race knows that was not the case.

British hopes for a medal in the men's 400-meter were dashed when on the far turn of the semifinal race, Redmond pulled up lame, apparently with a torn muscle. He tried to continue the race, but the pain forced him to stop. He stood there in agony, now out of competition but determined somehow to at least finish the race.

As he attempted to hobble toward the finish line, he seemed to reach the end of his strength with about one hundred meters still to go. At just that moment, a man from the stands ran up behind Derek, grabbed him around the waist, and began to support him and help him get to the finish line. It was his father, Jim Redmond.

As Derek realized who was holding him up and helping to propel him forward, his startled expression became a look of relief, and he was overcome with emotion. He grabbed his father around the neck, hugging him and crying as they moved together toward the finish line. With the crowd roaring their support for the two men, Derek finished the race.

Afterward, Derek said, "He was the only person who could have helped me, because he understood all I had been through."

THE HOLY ANGUISH THAT BRINGS US HOME

As we negotiate the course of life, sin makes all of us pull up lame in one way or another. If we're no longer seeking outright victory, we're at least struggling for a respectable showing. We still want to finish well and prove ourselves worthy and valuable, but our brokenness proves too big an obstacle. We stumble, we fall, we bleed. Then we stand up again, trying to summon renewed vigor and determination, vowing to show the world that we can do it!

However noble, this inner drive to turn in a good performance is no match for the destructive effects of living in the kingdom of self. We need a father who will run to us, grab us around the waist, and bring us to the finish line.

We have such a Father. He has climbed down out of the stands and has entered our selfish and broken arena. God, in the person of the Son, left the wonder of eternity to take on the form of a man, showing us just how much He cares. Jesus Christ came to our world to heal the brokenhearted, to save those who were lost, and to lift high those who have been beaten down by the oppression and destruction of sin.

It wasn't easy, and it wasn't clean. It was a holy anguish that brought us home, as Paul writes in Romans 5:7-8,

> In human experience it is a rare thing for one man to give his life for another, even if the latter be a good

man, though there have been a few who have had the courage to do it. Yet the proof of God's amazing love is this: that it was *while we were sinners* that Christ died for us. (PH)

For most of us, it comes as no surprise to hear that the answer to our plight is found in the death of God's Son. We know that Jesus Christ came to earth to die for our sins. The Bible states this plainly: "For God so loved the world that he gave his one and only Son, that whoever believes in him shall not perish but have eternal life" (John 3:16).

There are two basic ways to hear the message of this familiar passage. The most obvious way is through the head, by acknowledging the theological truth and spiritual "solution" of the cross of Christ. We hear the good news, and we want to be assured that God will allow us into heaven, so the logic of the cross makes sense. Millions who affirm the Christian faith intellectually assent to this historical fact: Jesus Christ died for their sins.

A second, and probably more important, way to hear this truth is through the heart, by realizing that not only did God provide a logical solution to the dilemma I face in sin, *He did something about my condition.* The Creator chose not to leave me stranded by my selfishness and rebellion, but to invade human history. The cost was immeasurable, for He willingly accepted the suffering of incredible scorn, humiliation, and pain, even to the point of death, in order to bring me home to the Kingdom of God. The "passion of Christ" is what we call His death—a bloody, brutal, and horrific event. We have been bought with the greatest of anguish.

Do you want to know the passion of Christ personally? Then listen with your heart:

Then the governor's soldiers took Jesus into the Praetorium and gathered the whole company of soldiers around him. They stripped him and put a scarlet robe on him, and then twisted together a crown of thorns and set it on his head. They put a staff in his right hand and knelt in front of him and mocked him. "Hail, king of the Jews!" they said. They spit on him, and took the staff and struck him on the head again and again. After they had mocked him, they took off the robe and put his own clothes on him. Then they led him away to crucify him. (Matthew 27:27-31)

Crucifixion is one of the cruelest, most painful forms of execution ever devised. It would often take several hours for Roman prisoners to die, because most died of suffocation when they finally ran out of strength to lift themselves up one more time to breathe. Prisoners were led to a public road to serve as an example of what happened when people dared cross the might of Rome. Jesus' mode of death was not unique—to the authorities He was just another enemy of the state. The uniqueness of His death lies in one simple fact: He was the only person in the history of humanity who was totally innocent of any crime.

The world's only sinless man hung like an animal, choking, gagging, calling out to His Father in pain and utter loneliness. The reason He was on that cross is also the reason He invaded our world. He loved us far too much to let us drift away. Our sentence for leaving Him was death, and we had already been declared guilty for setting up our own kingdom. So He came and suffered and died to take on our penalty. Jesus Christ died for us, and now we can be forgiven for all we have done, or will do, in denying His rightful place as King of our lives.

FROM THE KINGDOM OF SELF
TO THE KINGDOM OF GOD

My head had always known this—what is referred to as the gospel—or at least the gist of it anyway. I had been raised in church, and I knew that, as they say, God loved me and had a plan for my life. But my heart felt its power over a six-month period, culminating in one explosive night.

I was sitting by myself on some rocks overlooking British Columbia's Jervis Inlet, a hundred miles from Vancouver. It was close to midnight, and I had just heard a detailed description of the crucifixion. The man who had spoken to us that night, Jim Shelton, not only presented the information surrounding the cross and its theological implications, he introduced me to the heart of God. When Jim spoke, the love of Jesus bored into my soul as I watched Him suffer, bleed, and die—for me.

God touched me as I sat outside looking up at the stars. I instantly knew I was on holy ground, and I wept. Something deep inside me gave way, and a Voice called out to me, *You are My own special child! You will always be Mine!* I don't know how long I sat, but I have never been the same. I was touched by grace, defined as unmerited favor. The unmerited was obvious; the favor was yet to be grasped. Nevertheless, I leapt from the kingdom of self to the Kingdom of God.

A few years later I was again swept up by the power of the cross. Spending the summer between my junior and senior years of college playing guitar with a friend in a Waikiki nightclub, I was struggling with the future. One late-night walk after work, I knew God was there with me. I had been a believer for several years, even in ministry, but this night was different. As I considered how I had been living my life, I knew that if the gospel was true there had to be something more for me. That night I was again overpowered by God's love for me, and I moved closer to recognizing where I was still running my own show, and I stepped deeper into the Kingdom of God.

There have been many such times since. They are not always spectacular, or even extraordinary. Sometimes as I watch my children at play, or hear a song, or look into my wife's eyes, or gaze at the Colorado mountains, I am overwhelmed with the incredible love that God has for me. And I am drawn away from my need to perform and pulled deeper into desiring the Kingdom.

Throughout all of this I have come to believe that hearing and responding to the grace of God is a two-part process. The first is the initial decision of consciously and willingly leaving behind the kingdom of self and following Jesus Christ as King, thus entering into the relationship that leads to eternal life. This is what is meant by "becoming a Christian," when we first say yes to God and desire to love, serve, and follow Jesus.

I honestly believe that this is the one essential and necessary decision in the search for peace with God. Without some initial life step of desire and commitment, there can be no relationship, and thus no true healing. This is not to say that conservative Christianity has cornered the market because of the all-too-common insistence on the "right" words and a formal declaration of commitment. I have known many sincere and devout followers of the biblical Jesus who cannot point to a certain date, but they know they are His. I also know people of very different theological and traditional backgrounds who seem to have an identical sense of relationship with the Kingdom of Jesus, but they simply talk about it differently. Our walls have been built so high that many of us have lost Jesus as we try so hard to defend our particular view of Him. I assure you, God does not need us to defend Him; He wants us to be His ambassadors in His desire to reconcile the world to Himself.

This doesn't mean that there isn't a need for apologetics, the study of providing a rational case for faith. In this area we are not defending God per se; we are simply explaining the reality of God's love to the skeptic. If our attitude, demeanor, and delivery is compassionate and gentle, then an apologetic approach to sharing our joy brings God honor. But if we feel the need to put up our fists in pitched battle with anyone who would disagree or even challenge us, I believe we do the gospel a disservice.

FOLLOWING JESUS IN THE REAL WORLD

Sometimes the initial step of faith is so emphasized that it seems there's little else to the Christian faith—as if once we're "saved" we have somehow "made it" and there's little more to do. But I believe that this initial step is when the reality of the gospel initiates the healing process. For most of us, the real battle begins as we seek to grow in our willingness to *live* as one who loves, serves, and follows Jesus.

I used to think that when I met the woman I wanted to marry, all of my dating hurts, troubles, and frustrations would go away. I assumed that once I got married, *of course* I would always want to please my wife and seek her best! Oh, sure, there would probably be minor adjustments along the way, but the hard part would be over.

Was I ever wrong! Once Dee and I passed beyond the superficiality of dating and entered marriage, we were in the *real* world of relationships. When one of us got mad, we couldn't just walk away; somehow we had to figure out how to achieve resolution. When a conflict or disagreement cropped up, we could no longer sweep it under the rug; we had to deal with it or our relationship would go downhill fast.

Learning to live as a married person was like stepping through a door from Dorothy's black-and-white farm in Kansas into the dazzling colors of Munchkinland. The brilliant hues of the new world were so much more beautiful and alive than the old—but the painful glare of failures were all the more frightening. I wouldn't trade this new world for anything, but it's not what I had expected.

This process is what Paul refers to when he counsels, "Therefore, my dear friends, as you have always obeyed—not only in my presence, but now much more in my absence—continue to work out your salvation with fear and trembling, for it is God who works in you to will and to act according to his good purpose" (Philippians 2:12-13). I know many believers who don't like this passage. "Fear and trembling" before God conjures up a negative image. But to move from living for ourselves to living with Jesus as Lord is to move from black-and-white to color. The magnitude of the heavenly realm is filled with fury and spectacle. If we seek a God who loves us but doesn't call us to more than the world has to give, we will miss the power, majesty, and richness of the Kingdom.

And here is precisely where most of us live and breathe as believers: We have intellectually assented to the gospel and even committed ourselves to living in the Kingdom of God. But when it comes to actually *doing* it, it scares the living day-lights out of us! It requires us to turn our backs on everything we have been brought up to believe—the need to take care of ourselves, the importance of performing well enough to make it in this world—by trusting God in every nook and cranny of our lives. Of course it feels like sheer lunacy! Simple belief in Jesus seems good and right, but it's quite a leap to yield to grace as a raging tide that sweeps through our lives, calling us to abandon our emotional hold on our personal goals, our friends and family, even our very lives.

Yes, it *is* quite a leap.

But it is the way God has set up His universe. He intended you to experience life in living color, with wild and free abandonment within the parameters of His love. He wants to bring you home, to overwhelm you with kindness, gentleness, and mercy. He wants you to let go of the need to perform, for it only keeps you from enjoying Him.

The pace is furious on the treadmill of performance, but grace has come to free you from its harsh demands. This freedom did not come cheap, and it was not easily purchased. It was a brutal and bloody day when Jesus died, but His death was the greatest statement of love you will ever receive.

Your Father has seen your struggle along life's course, and He has jumped out of the stands to reach you on the track. He is waiting for the chance to put His arms around you, to let you know that He is there, and to help you finish the race He has called you to run. Derek Redmond wept when he saw his father. What is your response?

9

WHAT DOES GRACE LOOK LIKE?

Despite everything I have learned and experienced about grace in my struggle with the performance illusion, I still find myself wondering now and then where God fits into all of this. I am overwhelmed by the love Jesus displayed on the cross, yet I also harbor a fearful resignation regarding the majesty and power of God—especially when I fail, and deserve God's anger and judgment. What does this "raging grace" look like, and how can it free me from the need to perform?

My first year in high school I played football. I wasn't a very large kid. In fact, I was one of the smallest on the team. But I needed attention badly enough that I would willingly hit people far larger than a young man of my size should. I played defensive back on the junior varsity, and we were pretty good.

One game especially stands out. My dad, who had worked his way up the corporate ladder at IBM (which, at least in our case, stood for "I've Been Moved"), worked long and hard hours while I was growing up, so he wasn't able to attend many of my games over the years. The morning of this particular game, an important one for our team, I asked him if he would be able to come. He told me he would try.

We played on Saturday afternoons just before the varsity games. This particular game, against our crosstown rival, was for the league championship and so a large crowd was on hand.

Toward the end of the game, we were winning by about a touchdown, but their offense was moving on us. Their main weapon was a huge, fast, mean, ugly tight end, and he was good! Their best play was this guy taking two steps, turning to catch a pass, and then running like mad until four or five of us jumped on his back screaming, forcing him to fall. They had discovered that although our defensive backs were eager, none of us was very big, and so they were driving to the winning score.

With a minute to go, we had them stalled on our twenty-yard line, fourth down and four yards to go. Our coach, in a flash of characteristic ineptitude, called an all-out blitz, expecting them to fake to "Mongo" and pass the ball long. I was told to watch this guy, "just in case" — all by myself! When Mongo lined up, he looked me square in the eye, as if to say, "Say your prayers, boy!" I did.

As the ball was snapped, sure enough, the play was a short pass to the tight end, and I saw it coming all the way. Just as the quarterback released the ball, I closed my eyes and hit Mongo with everything I had.

I missed.

But, somehow, I missed so far that my helmet hit Mongo's hands. The ball popped up, one of our guys ran underneath it, and twenty-one guys started running down the field, with one little defensive back holding his head and going in circles.

The crowd was yelling, and all eyes were on the play as it headed down field. But somewhere, out of the middle of the crowd, I heard a lone voice cry out, "Way to go, Chappie!"

My dad had come to the game! He was up there in the middle of the stands waving and shouting to me. I started waving and shouting back to him . . . what a moment!

Not only had he come to my game, he had come for one purpose—to watch me play! He was not there to analyze the game, or to critique my performance, or to make a mild showing of support. He sacrificed his plans for the day to let me know that he cared for me, that he was my greatest fan, and that of all the players on the field, he was watching *me*.

GOD'S LOVE IS ENCOURAGING

Romans 8:31 says, "If God is for us, who can be against us?" To understand grace, you need to realize that God is personally committed to being your fan. Every minute of every day His thoughts are on you. Whenever you worry about a meeting, He is right there beside you, cheering you on, rubbing your back, assuring you that He is more than able to be there for you. When you are lonely, sad, frustrated, His resolve is calm, His focus clear, as He gently whispers for you to trust Him and let go of the emotions that sap energy and evaporate wisdom. His dedication to love, guide, and protect you can never be thwarted by your performance. No matter what you do, His love is your encouragement.

His encouragement is not based on a subjective response to how well you do, or look, or think. God is *for* you! His love is encouraging because He is madly in love with you, and He knows how badly you need to be freed from the insecurity and guilt that have paralyzed you. God is your biggest fan!

GOD'S LOVE IS PASSIONATE

One look at the life of Jesus reveals a side of God's character that has always made religious people nervous. It's no different now than it was two thousand years ago, but today it seems that current teaching seeks to whitewash the truth about Jesus.

Take the wedding at Cana in John 2, for example. There is a branch of the church—actually a few pastors and teachers, but enough to be significant—that has the audacity to teach that the wine Jesus miraculously furnished as a wedding present was merely grape juice, or unfermented wine. Nothing in the context of that event gives the slightest hint of that conclusion, and yet the teaching continues to this day. Why? Because religious people don't like to believe that Jesus drank alcohol. It doesn't fit their preconceived notions.

From all objective indications, however, moderate alcohol consumption was part of Jesus' life and a practice among early leaders of the Church. The warning was always against "much wine" and drunkenness, never a prohibition of alcohol for every believer.[1] In Jesus' day, alcohol in moderation was an integral part of celebration. Because of what it has done to many in our culture it may be wise and loving to abstain, but to rewrite Scripture to fit one particular view is to deny the historical realities of Jesus' life.

Why, then, is this such a fiery issue? Because religious people are more concerned with rules and regulations and control than they are with the fascinating person God has revealed in Jesus Christ. But God proves to us that conventional religious norms are not necessarily where God lives. Jesus, you see, was passionate about life. "The thief comes only to steal and kill and destroy," He said; "I have come that they may have life, and have it to the full" (John 10:10). He was so excited about life that He was accused of being a wild man, and He let us in on His attitude toward that charge when He said,

> "To what can I compare this generation? They are like children sitting in the marketplaces and calling out to others:
> "'We played the flute for you,

> and you did not dance;
> we sang a dirge,
> and you did not mourn.'
> For John came neither eating nor drinking, and they
> say, 'He has a demon.' The Son of Man came eating
> and drinking, and they say, 'Here is a glutton and a
> drunkard, a friend of tax collectors and "sinners."'
> But wisdom is proved right by her actions." (Matthew
> 11:16-19)

In the life of Jesus, whether in the way He talked, in the way He enjoyed people and gatherings, or in His passionate cleansings of the temple (see John 2 and Matthew 21, the first during His first public Passover, the second during His last), we see God's passion for life.

Our God is not a meek and predictable little deity. Take human sexuality, for example. God does not look away and blush in embarrassment. Our God invented sex, and fun, and laughter, and music, and mirth. We have some inkling of His passion in those times when in the midst of joyous celebration we feel a spark, a quickening of the heart, a rush of fresh air reminding us that we have been made from the divine cloth. This spark is no mistake, and God is not thrown off by our passion. Just the opposite is true—God is far more zealous, passionate, and fun than we could ever hope to be.

When we are living in a state of constant worry and stress over our ability to perform, we aren't free to *feel*. Our song becomes a dirge, our dance mechanical, and our laughter cheap and artificial. When we feel the breath of God on our skin we are like children on the last day of school—running, jumping, singing, shouting, "I am free, free, FREE!!"

GOD'S LOVE IS TENDER

Jesus Christ is majestic, powerful, encouraging, and passionate. But there is another side to His character—tenderness.

Tender is a wonderful word. What comes to your mind as you see it on the printed page? I recall a photo ad of a heavyweight wrestler cradling his infant child. Tender is the soft, gentle touch that cradles our frail hearts. Tender is comfort for the vulnerable, compassion for the hurting. I believe that we often neglect God's trait of all-encompassing tenderness toward His little ones.

I didn't always believe this. I had heard so much about God's anger and wrath, and about the awesome and majestic power of His holiness, that although I knew He loved us I didn't think He was much inclined to be sensitive and gentle when we messed up. That was during a time in my life when my faith was more a system than a relationship. God wanted me to know about Him, and His deepest desire was for my adherence to His laws and dictates. I was naive and arrogant enough to believe that, on my own, I was actually capable of fulfilling such a rigid expectation. *Others* messed up and made poor choices, and God in His ultimate holiness and judgment would deal with them, sometimes with expedience. But not me. I was a "committed disciple."

Slowly, though, I began to be aware of some chinks in my own armor. I started to realize how my own zealousness for God often slipped into arrogance and judgment. People who were critical of me, I used to think, were either misinformed or misunderstood my motives. But as time went on I met more and more people who reflected God's character more by their life than by their vocal convictions. I saw how my holiness was a cheap imitation of something deeper, something I had only begun to grasp. It took the courage of friends, a loving and honest wife, and many, many times of personal and spiritual struggle to show me how badly I had misunderstood the gospel. Then I knew I needed a tender God, for I realized that I was as big a sinner as the "other" guy.

My friend and pastor, Tom Melton, tells of the time his three-year-old son Brandon tried to surprise Tom by bringing him a big glass of milk. In the process, Brandon broke glasses, spilled milk all over the kitchen, and drenched Tom head to toe. As it dawned on Brandon that he might have botched the plan, Tom's eyes filled with tears as he was overwhelmed with love for his son. "True," Tom recalled, "he screwed up everything he touched. But he is my son, and I just couldn't stop thinking how much I loved him."

THE HEART OF A TENDER GOD

How does God deal with us when we mess up? Or, maybe a better question to ask is, What is God's heart toward someone who disobeys Him, denies His righteous standard, or makes a mockery of God's authority by sinning against Him and humanity? This is a critical question when I think about my need to perform. How can I truly be free if I am not free to fall — or at least to stumble — as I walk through life?

Jesus' encounter with the woman caught in adultery gives us a clue to the heart of God when we fall.

You can probably recall the event. Jesus was causing quite a stir in the temple that day, as everyone gathered around Him to hear Him teach. This put the Pharisees and teachers of the law out of business for the time being, and they didn't like it. So they decided to use a pawn — a wretched pawn at that. They tried to use a woman who had just been caught in the act of adultery to get to Jesus. In front of the entire crowd, they brought her and threw her at Jesus' feet.

"Moses told us to stone her . . . what do *you* say?" they asked, while a few silently snickered in the back. They thought they had Him. Here was Jesus, attracting all kinds of attention by preaching a message of freedom and love to the people. If He were to let this woman off scot-free, He would deny their traditional faith and be exposed as a fraud. But if He agreed to stone her, the people would rebel against Him, for He would show Himself to be more interested in law than mercy. They had Him.

But Jesus confounded their plans by doing the strangest

thing. He knew what they were up to, but I believe that His main concern at that moment was the woman. Here she was, caught, standing accused in the holiest place on earth, before all her people, guilty as charged. Imagine the humiliation and loneliness of being caught and singled out for death. Jesus, knowing that the eyes of the crowd were on her, hearing them shout rude and painful comments, wanted to protect her from this public display of hatred. So He bent down and started to doodle on the ground.

Everyone wondered what He was doing. But as He persisted, there was a noticeable shift in focus, a change in momentum. I believe that Jesus bent down to take the focus of the crowd off of that woman by placing it on Himself, a sign of what He would do on the cross for us all.

As Jesus rose, He said those famous words, "If any one of you is without sin, let him be the first to throw a stone at her" (John 8:7).

The beauty of this encounter is not so much Jesus' wisdom before the accusers as His incredible tenderness toward the woman. Even a cursory reading sparks unanswerable questions: Where was the man? Why wasn't his hide on the line, too? How did those religious leaders know just where to find a woman in the act of adultery at precisely that moment? Could they have been carrying her business card for future reference? What did Jesus write when he bent down?

The answers remain mere conjecture, but one thing is certain: the only issue the scribes and Pharisees cared about in this incident was indicting Jesus Christ. The woman was simply an object to be used and discarded.

But Jesus never answered them. He remained strangely silent. They continued to question Him, but He ignored them, as if He didn't even hear them. Why?

Because Jesus Christ is tender. In His eyes, this adulterous woman was a beautiful, precious, and wondrous masterpiece of His creation. Yes, she had walked away from His authority and His purity. Yes, she had failed.

Yes, she had broken the covenant of marriage and possibly destroyed a family. Her sin was terrible and costly. But Jesus Christ is tender. When He bent down to write, He had one thing in mind: to take the attention off her shame and guilt and focus it on Himself. Despite all of the evidence stacked against her, she was still His beloved child, made in His image, and He had come to let her know that no offense was too great to separate her from Himself. He was too deeply and desperately in love with her.

Once Jesus absorbed the glaring spotlight, the woman became a spectator in the great drama of the day. His command was awesome, His insight beyond human wisdom. In one brief statement Jesus turned the tide and reduced the lynch mob from religious arrogance to recognition of their common guilt. One minute they were calling for blood; the next minute they were slinking away under the weight of their own sinful and darkened hearts. The brilliance of that moment is not only Jesus' great tenderness for the woman, but His tenderness for us all, because He told each of us that we are no less and no more guilty.

As you throw off the bonds of your need to perform, you will discover that because Jesus Christ is tender you are *truly* free. No matter what you do, He will always be gentle with you. When you hurt someone or hurt yourself; when you cheat, or lie, or grab power; when you walk away from Him; He loves you no less. In His great love He is willing to take the guilt and shame off of you and place it on Himself in order to bring you back into His Kingdom.

GOD'S LOVE IS EXTRAVAGANT

My wife never does anything halfway. Whether it's a birthday, a holiday, the last day of school, or a simple "I'm glad you're in my life" celebration, she goes all out. More times than I can count I have walked out of a meeting somewhere, or my office, or off an airplane, to discover a party in progress. She and our kids will blow up balloons, make posters, hang streamers, and top it off with cards, gifts, and an incredible activity that celebrates our life together. No matter how preoccupied or busy I have been at the time, these have been some of our most cherished family times.

She doesn't *need* to go to all this trouble. She could just tell me that she loves me, and that she enjoys our life together. A card would probably do it, and an occasional phone message. But balloons? Streamers? Wacky and creative trinkets? Who needs that to know that they are important?

I do.

Because of her extravagant love, she has convinced me that she loves me *and* likes me for who I am. I may perform well, or I may mess up, but ultimately neither will change her love for me. I have no doubt that my wife is crazy about me. She repeatedly goes to extravagant lengths to prove it.

Just the fact that we are alive is evidence enough that the Lord cares about us. God doesn't *need* to go all out to convince us of our worth, but He does. Over and over again—with the beauty and wonder of creation, the miracle of birth, and music, and human love. When our eyes are opened by the freedom of the gospel, and we are able to stop being so self-focused and self-absorbed, it's easy to see that God is constantly throwing a party in our honor. Not because we have earned it, but because He *likes* us! The angels are *always* singing, the heavens are *always* opened, and the adventure of life is *always* surprising us. When in our complaints and worries we fail to see it, it's because we "have eyes but do not see."

Jesus' life was filled with celebration and extravagance. When He fed the five thousand, He had weeks of leftovers for them to take home. When He changed the water into wine at the wedding celebration, the master of ceremonies was amazed at the incredible quality of the wine. Jesus was repeatedly accused of being a partier and a rabble-rouser, of running with the wrong crowd. People were aghast at the way He scoffed at burdensome traditions, socialized with outcasts, and came into physical contact with lepers. He never backed down from living a quality of life that was foreign to His society. Whether it was His stroll on the waves or His complete and total cleansing of the temple courts, Jesus overdid it time and again. Perhaps this is what He meant when He said, "I have come that they may have life, and have it to the full" (John 10:10).

What comes to mind when you consider God? What do you see when you look at Jesus? Do you imagine a solemn, vengeful bureaucrat who is more interested in rules and form than in the abundance of life? Do you see a judicial monarch who maintains a detailed database on all of your thoughts and deeds, good *and* bad?

Or can you see another picture of God? A gentle man with his arms wrapped around a newly wakened little girl; a humble counselor sitting on a dusty road, softly stroking a pained and broken woman's hair as she pours out her suffering; a moon-streaked sky, filled with powerful clouds, and a raging sea, with a free and flowing figure dancing on the water.

Do you see heaven as a sullen, dour vastness where you are always cold? Or can you see the host of laughing, frolicking angels, singing and rejoicing with the King?

Jesus Christ is full of passion, joy, mirth, merriment, and as Brennan Manning has said, relentless tenderness. He is consumed with life, and His desire for you is without equal. You need not perform for Him, for He knows that you will live a much more productive and fruitful life when you are living out of freedom instead of guilt.

Despite stereotypes to the contrary, Jesus Christ is anything but mild, gently gliding across the fields with a little lamb riding His shoulders. But you may always rely on the truth that with all His passion and strength, He is tender and gentle and kind. He has pledged to you His commitment, loyalty, and love. You can trust Him, because He has proven over and over, ultimately by dying, how far He will go to let you know just how valuable you are.

10

WHAT MUST I DO TO BE SAVED?

The heart of the Christian message
is God Himself waiting for His redeemed children
to push into conscious awareness of His presence.
That type of Christianity which happens now
to be the vogue knows this Presence only in theory.
It fails to stress the Christian's privilege
of present realization. . . . Ignoble contentment takes
the place of burning zeal . . . for the most part,
we bother ourselves very little
about the absence of personal experience.

A. W. TOZER, *The Pursuit of God*

There is a vast difference between "ignoble contentment" and a "burning zeal" in a believer's relationship with God. In our culture it's a social disgrace to be perceived as burning with zeal. It's fine to believe in something, so long as you don't care too much. And the even greater sin is to be so consumed with passion that it spills over into another's "space." We have been so inoculated with a pluralistic world view that even the truth of the gospel is widely considered a relative, and therefore impotent, faith.

Yet no one in human history compares to Jesus Christ in the way He talked about Himself. Not Mohammed, not Confucius, not Alexander the Great. No major world religious or political leader ever went as far as Jesus in the audacious assertions He made about His identity, mission, and character—not even close! The declarations He made were beyond egocentric; without His deeds to back them up they would be grounds for incarceration. In speech as well as action, Jesus pointed to only one source of healing, holiness, peace, hope, and life—Himself. All four gospel writers have but one message in mind—to show the world that Jesus Christ is like no other.

The Apostle Paul sums up the centrality of the person of Jesus Christ in Colossians 1:15-17:

> He is the image of the invisible God, the firstborn over all creation. For by him all things were created: things in heaven and on earth, visible and invisible, whether thrones or powers or rulers or authorities; all things were created by him and for him. He is before all things, and in him all things hold together.

In Jesus, all of life comes into focus. And if He is right, then anything that runs contrary to Him must be wrong. As followers of Jesus, we are called to love, gentleness, and mercy in our relations with others. But that does not mean we must allow our faith to be dismissed as just another world view. Jesus Christ is the God who has come, and His message is a passionate plea for life itself, a life found only in trusting Him as Lord and King.

When I perform, I trust myself. But Jesus came to bring me healing and wholeness as I trust in Him, and whenever I attempt to dilute this message with the elitist and cavalier notion of philosophic pluralism, I take the heart right out of the gospel. The heart of the gospel proclaims that I belong to Jesus, and therefore I find freedom *only* as I trust in Him for security, identity, and fulfillment.

How, then, can I let go of my drive to perform? If trusting Jesus is not a matter of performance, what *does* God want from me? Jesus was asked this same question:

> When they found him on the other side of the lake, they asked him, "Rabbi, when did you get here?"
> Jesus answered, "I tell you the truth, you are looking for me, not because you saw miraculous signs but because you ate the loaves and had your

fill. Do not work for food that spoils, but for food that endures to eternal life, which the Son of Man will give you. On him God the Father has placed his seal of approval."

Then they asked him, "What must we do to do the works God requires?"

Jesus answered, "The work of God is this: to believe in the one he has sent." (John 6:25-29)

So the answer to our need for healing, for freedom, for peace, and for life is found in the word *believe*. But what does Jesus mean when He says we must believe in Him?

The most common understanding of the word *belief* is to make an intellectual assent to something, as in, "I believe the Broncos will eventually win a Super Bowl" (even though the idea may be neither remotely possible nor personally critical). This understanding of belief as intellectual assent is the primary reason for the defeated condition of many in the Church who wonder if the gospel holds any real power for today. But in the original language of the New Testament, the biblical word *believe* (from the Greek *pisteuo*) is better rendered in our current vernacular as "trust." What must we do in order to trust?

JUMPING FOR JESUS

Dee and I met each other in a beautiful camp in Northern California called Young Life's Woodleaf. One year I was there as the speaker, and one of my roles was to belay every camper the forty feet to the ground at the end of the ropes course, thus giving me a unique one-on-one experience with every kid.

This particular year we had a blind girl as a camper. She was sharp, fun, and vocal, and she was determined not to let her blindness keep her from having the week of her life. Even on the ropes course, where she had to go through rigorous and difficult maneuvers with a guide on either side of her, she was loud and funny. But when she got to me, it was a different story.

She knew that this final event was the hardest part of the course, because she had listened intently to others who had been through it. She also knew that after climbing fifteen additional feet on some small boards nailed to a tree she would have to stand on a small ledge, with the only props to keep her safe a thin belay line and me. She and I had built a solid friendship by that time, but right then it was definitely strained.

After several minutes of my explanation, her soul-searching and tears, she appeared ready to jump for the bar, suspended a few feet from the platform, hovering at about forty feet from the ground. She suddenly stopped, inclined her head toward my general direction, and said, "I can't do this!"

"Trust me. I'll catch you. I promise," I replied.

"But I can't see you."

"I know," I replied, "but I can see you. Trust me."

She jumped.

When she reached the ground and felt the strong arms of the summer staff assistant around her, keeping her from falling, she started to cry. I scrambled out of my harness and ran to meet her. As soon as she realized who was standing beside her, she clung to me like a cross between a rescued hostage and a terrified child, sobbing, "That was great! That was great!"

If we really believe—that is, trust—that Jesus Christ is crazy about us just as we are, not as we think we're *supposed* to be, then we will be on the road to recovery. So many say they "believe" in Jesus while remaining convinced that there is more to it. There isn't. The only thing that is required of us is to depend on Jesus for all that we are. This is not performance; it's reliance. The focus is no longer on *me*; it is on Jesus. When I rely on Jesus for healing and wholeness, looking to Him for freedom from the bondage of performance, I no longer live out of an "ought-to" legalism. Instead, I am free to respond to my Lord in love.

Some may protest, But won't this view of grace lead to spiritual sloth? Don't people need leaders and teachers to direct their steps and provide them with expectations, norms, and regulations to ensure their lifestyle is "worthy" of Christ? This is the generally accepted viewpoint, but it has troubling elements.

This view implies that, given a choice, people will generally take the easiest route. When presented with the freedom to choose, they will be lazy, selfish, and insincere. Therefore, leaders must tell them to do what is in their best interests. Can you see how this view encourages the need to perform? It emphasizes the duty of obedience, with fear and guilt as motivators, rather than the freedom of responding to Jesus in love.

For a few years I taught a seminary class on strategic planning to parachurch students. In preparation for this class I read many different books on leadership, which helped me view leadership from a new perspective. The best book I read was *Leadership Is an Art*, by Max DePree. Because God made us in His image, DePree said we "covet inclusiveness . . . each of us is needed. Each of us has a gift to bring. Each of us is a social being and our institutions are social units. Each of us has a deep-seated desire to contribute."[1] The Apostle Paul puts it this way, "For we are God's workmanship, created in Christ Jesus to do good works, which God prepared in advance for us to do" (Ephesians 2:10).

There is a fine line between being honest and loving in our critique of others and lording it over them with our misuse of power. Believers should care enough to help others to see their weaknesses, to point out where they may be in the wrong position for their gifts and talents, and to "speak the truth in love" (Ephesians 4:15), regardless of position and lines of authority.

But this kind of guidance must be carried out within the context of community, and from a foundation of sincere love. A community or leader who imposes nonbiblical expectations on others from "above" denies God's desire that love be our motivation and empowerment for holy living.

Some may fear that this freedom of love is dangerous. After all, the argument states, given a chance at selfishness most will take advantage of others. The Kinsey report, for example, indicated that 40 percent of married American men had been involved in an extramarital affair. Some estimates are even higher. It's been suggested that the rise of sexual infidelity in the United States is due to the "freedom" granted by our cultural anonymity. People can do and act as they wish because in our busy, crowded world they can hide their secrets, thus proving this theory of the danger of granting too much freedom.

But does the internal freedom of love lead us to cast all that we believe in and hold dear to the wind? Hardly. In fact, just the opposite is true. What drives us to moral failure, to denying commitments, to laziness in our daily tasks, is *our neglect of the truth of God's love for us*. We break our moral commitments because we think our choices will bring us greater freedom and happiness. We turn our backs on those we love because we think we can find *more* love with someone else—forgetting that no person can ever meet our every need. We take the easy way out in our jobs, hanging in there simply for the paycheck, because we have no sense of calling or purpose.

These issues of personal freedom can all be traced to a single, crucial choice: either I am living the grand adventure, trusting Jesus Christ who loves me and calls me by name, or I am struggling through life trying to live it on my own. If I honestly believe that I am a special, uniquely blessed, and gifted child of God, then I can live with joy, freedom, and purpose. Out of this comes a new holiness, for I am free to live as God has called me. I no longer base my identity on my performance, and I no longer carry the guilt of non-performance.

We need not live in fear and guilt: "We may approach the throne of grace with fullest confidence, that we may receive mercy for our failures and grace to help in the hour of need" (Hebrews 4:16, PH). We have been asked to trust the Voice who continually calls us by name, who cheers us on to greater adventures and newness of life, who never wanders off or loses sight of us, who summons us to jump, to trust, to dance with Him. Oh, that we could experience the Kingdom of God as jumping into the outstretched arms of the Almighty, grabbing His neck when we finally land, sobbing and laughing all at once, "That was great! That was great!"

PART THREE

Performing for God Versus Responding to God's Love

Therefore, there is now no condemnation for those
who are in Christ Jesus, because through Christ Jesus
the law of the Spirit of life set me free
from the law of sin and death. . . .
Those who live according to the sinful nature have their
minds set on what that nature desires; but those who live
in accordance with the Spirit have their minds set on what
the Spirit desires. The mind of sinful man is death,
but the mind controlled by the Spirit is life and peace;
the sinful mind is hostile to God. It does not submit
to God's law, nor can it do so. Those controlled
by the sinful nature cannot please God.
You, however, are not controlled by the sinful nature
but by the Spirit, if the Spirit of God lives in you.
And if anyone does not have the Spirit of Christ,
he does not belong to Christ. But if Christ is in you,
your body is dead because of sin, yet your spirit is alive
because of righteousness.

ROMANS 8:1-2,5-10

The conflict between flesh and spirit is the experience
of all who begin the spiritual life by the influx of God's
life-giving word. Sometimes the conflict is long, sometimes
short. The disciplines for the spiritual life, rightly under-
stood, are time-tested activities consciously undertaken
by us as new men or women to allow our spirit
ever-increasing sway over our embodied selves. They help
by assisting the ways of God's Kingdom to take the place
of the habits of sin embedded in our bodies.

DALLAS WILLARD
The Spirit of the Disciplines

107

11

WHAT DO I BELIEVE?

When we lived in Southern California, Dee and I were given two incredible gifts. The first was from Tony, a former student we had cared for while he was in school. He had been given a fairly large sum of money from a family trust when he turned twenty-one. As he prayed about how to invest this money for his future, he made the decision to lend our family over ninety thousand dollars so that we could purchase our first house. Even in 1983, this was the kind of money it took just to begin thinking about owning a home in the community where we were ministering to kids and families through Young Life.

The second gift we received came from Mike, a friend and volunteer leader in Young Life who was an independent contractor. His business entailed buying older, run-down, fixer-upper homes in expensive areas, gutting them, and building in their place beautiful large houses. As Mike advised us in choosing a home, he offered to help us by getting us into that kind of a house and donating his time for two to three months as we worked together to remodel it. Needless to say we were humbled by the depth of love and commitment we received from these two men.

The house we bought was perfect—it had a terrible layout from haphazard additions, the lawn had not been mowed in years, the carpet was threadbare, and it smelled so bad that Dee and I tore up the carpet in the entire house the first night we moved in. Mike and I had our work cut out for us.

We found that to create something beautiful from an existing house is more arduous than it sounds. We had neither the time nor the money to level it and start from scratch. We had to use what was there and modify what we could, keep what we had to, and live with the result.

Months later when we were finally finished, we ended up owning a warm, comfortable home that reflected our family's tastes and Dee's gift of hospitality. It didn't happen overnight, and we encountered many setbacks along the way. Sometimes we were so discouraged that we were ready to give up and go back to our apartment—which wasn't a house, but it was a whole lot easier to deal with. Although it was hard work to rebuild a house, when all was said and done we were glad we had hung in there.

Rebuilding a faith system that accurately reflects biblical truth and frees us from the need to perform is also hard work. It may mean the unraveling of years of misunderstanding, false teaching, oppressive leadership, and other hidden yet influential forces.

You may find that it will mean honestly confronting in yourself some inbred prejudices against others, yourself, or even God. As you examine the core of your personal faith, you might discover that the God you have tried to serve and follow is not the God revealed in the life of Jesus. You may find out that, despite what you have always thought, you *are* valuable, lovable, and ultimately worthy, not because of what you have accomplished, but because of your heritage as the pinnacle of creation.

The process that Dee and I went through in rebuilding a house is similar to the process we must all go through if we honestly seek to know what God wants for us.

ASSESSING YOUR SITUATION

The first step in the process of rebuilding a house is taking inventory of what you have: deciding what's good that you want to keep and determining what needs to be changed, fixed, or thrown out. The same is true when rebuilding a faith system. We must be honest about the foundational truths that we count on to undergird our convictions.

If, for example, you have a hidden yet compelling belief that God is unapproachable, everything else you believe will be viewed through that lens. Or if you fundamentally believe that God's primary concern is your happiness, issues such as spiritual discipline and obedience may have little impact.

The following test is a tool to help you think through what you believe. Take a few minutes to answer each question by circling the response that most closely matches the first thing that comes to your mind. If you can be honest about what you *really* think, you may be well on the road to building the kind of faith system that reflects what you actually believe to be true.

WHAT DO I BELIEVE?
Please circle the answer that first comes to mind as being the most appropriate. There are no wrong answers, because every answer comes directly from Scripture.
   1. Which of these words best describe God's basic character to you?
   A. Powerful
   B. Gentle
   C. Passionate
   D. Just

2. I think that when God thinks about me, He is . . .
   A. Mildly interested
   B. Disappointed
   C. Ecstatic
   D. Frustrated
3. God is most concerned about . . .
   A. My obedience
   B. My giving
   C. My love for him
   D. My consistency
4. The most important aspect of my Christian life is . . .
   A. Knowing God
   B. Caring for others
   C. Loving God
   D. Being good
5. If I were to explain faith to someone I would say . . .
   A. "You are a sinner in need of a Savior."
   B. "God wants to use you."
   C. "God likes you."
   D. "God has a plan for your life."
6. If God were to say just one audible sentence to me right now, it would be . . .
   A. "Know the Truth, for the Truth will set you free."
   B. "Give as I have given to you."
   C. "You are My beloved child, in whom I am well pleased."
   D. "Live according to My Word."
7. The reason I pray is . . .
   A. Because Jesus has told me to.
   B. To set loose the Spirit of God.
   C. To draw near to the heart of God.
   D. To remember to whom I belong.
8. The title I believe most accurately describes Jesus Christ is . . .

A. King
B. Counselor
C. Friend
D. Lord

SELF-TEST EVALUATION

There are many ways to categorize and systematize the Christian faith. Believers over the centuries have attempted to describe the God of the Bible in terms and concepts that make sense to them.

There is always the danger, however, of bringing into the discussion our predisposed viewpoints and historical biases. Our convictions, lifestyles, and belief systems are inevitably influenced in some way by our environment. Factors as diverse as family history, educational background, and empirical experience all impact what we believe to be true about life. No person's faith system is immune to these influences.

But God has given us the gift of Scripture—an accurate historical record of the early followers of Jesus Christ. If the source of truth for the modern believer is the Bible, it is imperative that we do all we can to study it with the most open perspective possible.

How we view God and how we think He views us directly influence how we build our own faith system. The "What Do I Believe?" self-test provides four distinct ways of understanding the Christian faith. Each of the four views is represented in the letter groups of the responses as follows:

A answers. These represent believers who seek to discover the essence of Truth and live accordingly. You believe that God is most concerned with our obedience, that He is distant and powerful, and that life is basically a series of choices based on our knowledge. Truth and adherence to that truth is ultimately what matters most.

B answers. These represent believers who consider Jesus'

example the bottom line of faith, and whose goal is to give of themselves to others. For you, God is primarily interested in giving, and so we too are called to give of ourselves.

C *answers.* These responses represent believers who affirm that God's greatest desire is to be in relationship with them. Although you agree that the other three views are important aspects of the Christian faith, you believe they are secondary and even consequential to this basic understanding.

D *answers.* These represent believers who view God as a kind of "accountant-in-the-sky," chiefly concerned with their consistency. You know that God has a plan, and it is your job as a Christian to live up to the demands of that plan. You may occasionally slip and fall, but the good you do must far outweigh the bad for you to please God.

None of these views is mutually exclusive, and few people answer the questions across the board according to one viewpoint, but for most believers a clear pattern emerges.

As you evaluate your responses, see if they fall generally into one or two systems. Perhaps it is only a question or two that gives you a clue to what you actually believe or shows you where your inconsistencies are. Reflect on what you were thinking and feeling as you responded. Then take a few moments to consider what you honestly believe to be the foundational truth of biblical faith, according to the way you answered the questions.

This book has attempted to present a case for category C, which affirms that God's basic plan is to be in an intimate and authentic relationship with each of us based upon *His* work of grace. Although you may acknowledge this in your head, and even if you selected C answers for the majority of your responses, there may be areas of your life in which you actually believe that either God is too soft to take seriously, too untouchable to be bothered, or too disappointed to be faced. Assessing these areas of your faith system is the first critical step in finding freedom from the hold of the performance illusion.

FORMING A PLAN

When Mike and I teamed up to rebuild our house, the next step after assessing our situation was to formulate a plan. We had to determine what we wanted to do, how much money and energy it would cost, and whether we were willing and able to follow through. The incentive to keep going was the knowledge that Dee and I could not live in the house as it was when we purchased it. But actually going through the process of planning what it would take to make it our home was a difficult and sobering experience. We had gone far enough to know what we wanted (and needed) to do; now we had to prepare ourselves to make it happen.

To rebuild a faith system is costly. Simply *wanting* God's love to motivate us and free us from the need to perform doesn't mean we know how to get there. It is extremely difficult to wipe away all of the years and messages of the performance illusion.

We might be able to say the right words: "I am not going to live under the oppression of the need to perform. I will let God love me as I am and not as I am supposed to be, and I will treat my failures as I treat my successes, for they are nothing compared to the surpassing love that God has for me." We might even believe all of this to be true, intellectually.

But it is here that the battle begins in earnest, for everything inside of us will fight this truth. It is sin that says, "But *I* want to win, *I* want to make an impact." The inner voice wants so desperately to be recognized for personal achievement that to enter the presence of God with nothing but ourselves to make us worthy seems an outrage. And yet the Scriptures teach nothing else, for we cannot begin to please and glorify God on our own terms.

Sue Monk Kidd, when encountering this same struggle, spent a long, lonely night in search of the truth:

> I closed the Bible, feeling the deep click of truth that comes when God reaches out in startling ways from its pages. We seem to think that God speaks by seconding the ideas that we have already adopted, but God nearly always catches us by surprise. If it's God's Spirit blowing, someone ends up having feathers ruffled in an unforeseen way. God tends to confound, astonish, and flabbergast. A Bethlehem stable, a Roman cross, an empty garden tomb. We might as well reconcile ourselves to the fact that God's truth often turns up in ways we don't expect.[1]

The secret of rebuilding your faith system is to continually remind yourself of a startling truth: God is crazy about you. And no amount of praying, of service, of preaching, of money, of giving, or of sacrifice will ever make God love you more than He does right now. Every time you hear a message that whispers to you that while God may love you, you sure could be doing more to be a more productive Christian, dive deep into the well of the Spirit. There God waits to wrap His arms of grace around you as He sings you a gentle lullaby. Freedom is not in the trying harder; it is in the letting go.

All of Scripture points to Jesus Christ as the Center around which all of life revolves. He is the focal point, the beginning and the end. Knowing that He knows all about me, and loves me, and even likes me, is like air to the drowning and food to the starving. There is nothing else. Not my love for Him, but it is His love for me that gives me joy, meaning, and freedom to experience life as He intended it.

Henri Nouwen has said that we all go through life asking the question, "Who am I?"[2] We spend every day trying to find the answer to this question of self-identity. We may not recognize it or want to admit it, but in our work, in our play, and in our relationships we are constantly on the prowl for clues in our central search to discover, "Who am I?"

There are three basics messages we try to grab on to in this search. They are contained in the following statements:

1. "I am what I do." I am an executive, a salesman, a homemaker, an athlete, a minister, a counselor. I am valuable because I make a contribution that matters. I have trophies on my mantle, a gold watch, a plaque that reminds me that I am important. My work and my accomplishments are my life. I spend most of my day hoping that someone will come along and notice how much I accomplish, and therefore how valuable I am.

2. "I am what I control." I have a house, a car, some people who work for me, some children, a church staff, a budget. See who I am? I am important because I have these all under my control and authority. I am valuable because without me they would not function properly. This is why I control and exert my influence and power over others, because this is where I matter.

3. "I am what others say about me." My name is all I have that is ultimately mine. Therefore I must do all I can to protect my name. Even if I fail, I must seek to keep my name from being destroyed or taken from me. As I walk the streets and hallways, I listen for the whispers about me, and I silently plead for them to be fair, to be kind. As I make decisions and make impressions I must constantly be aware that people might not like me, or might speak ill of me, and so I must be very careful not to risk who I am, for what they say about me is everything.

But each of these statements is in fact an illusion, Nouwen says, for it will never satisfy the longing of the soul for that inner voice who releases us from the need to perform. When we attempt to find our place by doing or controlling or worrying about what other people will say, we are at others' mercy—and therefore we cannot escape disappointment. When everything that gives us our reason for being is based on how we perform, there is no hope of escape from the performance illusion.

REKINDLING THE FIRE OF FREEDOM

There is only one way to rekindle the spark of freedom that will thaw the frigid requirements of performance — to realize that our identity has already been given to us, and we have only to live it.

When Jesus emerged from the Jordan after His baptism, the voice of the Father thundered from the heavens for all to hear, "You are my Son, whom I love; with you I am well pleased" (Luke 3:22). If you have responded to the call of God in your life by choosing to follow Jesus Christ as your King and Lord, and by making the decision to enter the Kingdom of God as a new creation, God proudly gives you a new name, which is rooted in Him. God says to you, "You are My child, whom I love; with you I am well pleased!"

This name, *the Beloved of God,* is the place of refuge for every child of God. It is the source of your identity. When you are tempted to fall back into searching for your value in what you do, what you control, and what others say about you, run to Him and listen for His voice. Remember that in Christ you have a new name. The answer to your question "Who am I?" can only be found in your name, *the Beloved of God.* The message that your identity can be found in how you perform is a lie. You are the Beloved; never let anyone take that beautiful truth away from you.

To rebuild a faith system that will give you the strength to withstand pressure to perform and listen to the gentle voice of God, you will need to commit yourself to specific action. The next four chapters will present some practical steps for getting off the performance treadmill. All they are, however, are ways of hearing Jesus say to you, "Come to me, all you who are weary and burdened, and I will give you rest" (Matthew 11:28).

12

RESPONDING TO GOD'S LOVE IN MY FAITH

As long as we have only a vague inner feeling of discontent
with our present way of living, and only an indefinite
desire for "things spiritual,"
our lives will continue to stagnate in a generalized
melancholy. We often say, "I am not very happy.
I am not content with the way my life is going. I am not
really joyful or peaceful, but I just don't know how things
can be different, and I guess I have to be realistic and
accept my life as it is." It is this mood of resignation that
prevents us from actively searching for the life of the Spirit.
Our first task is to dispel the vague, murky feeling
of discontent and to look critically at how we are living our
lives. This requires honesty, courage,
and trust. We must honestly unmask and courageously
confront our many self-deceptive games. We must trust
that our honesty and courage will lead us not to despair,
but to a new heaven and a new earth.

HENRI J. M. NOUWEN, *Making All Things New*

I have attempted to show that while to many people life is a series of performances for various audiences, the life God has called us to is free from the need to perform for anybody. God desires us to respond freely and enthusiastically to His initiative of love.

What does this mean in the most basic aspect of our lives as believers: responding to God's love in our faith? How would our practical, everyday life look different if our relationship to Christ reflected a response to grace rather than a need to perform?

Like many believers, you may be living with a set of unspoken yet clearly expected rules and disciplines that you feel are necessary to fulfill in order to please God. These external requisites of the traditional Christian experience may be all that you have known, and they may have had a positive effect on you and your faith.

On the other hand, as many believers have experienced, you may feel that these disciplines and expectations have been defeating and de-energizing. Because of the human tendency to hold more tightly to rules and doctrines than to Jesus, the "rules for living the successful Christian life" may have been more a burden than a help to you. Don't let that stop you from taking time to reexamine what spiritual disciplines can mean to you as you seek to respond to the love God has for you as His child. The traditional disciplines of the faith are wonderful God-given tools to help us grow in our love for Jesus—so long as they are rooted in freedom, not in duty.

In recent decades, evangelical attitudes toward the spiritual disciplines as a means to growth in Christ seem to have cooled. Dallas Willard addresses this issue in his classic book *Spirit of the Disciplines:*

> Most conservatives [believers] by the early seventies generally accepted that being a Christian had nothing essentially to do with *actually* following or being like Jesus. It was readily admitted that most "Christians" did not really follow him and were not really like him. "Christians aren't perfect, just forgiven" became a popular bumper sticker. The only absolute requirement for being a Christian was that one believe the proper things *about* Jesus.[1]

This tendency continues today, as many sincere and devout believers wonder if a life committed to loving and following Jesus is even possible. The question we must ask, then, is "What does an authentic and realistic faith look like?" How can someone who wants to be free of the religious performance ethic live out faith in Jesus Christ?

The good news is that it is possible to live a life committed to an active and vibrant lifestyle within the Kingdom of God. And more than that, the path to get us there is not new;

it involves recapturing the essence of biblical Christianity. What we see and read and experience in our culture—a frantic and futile attempt to please a disappointed God through external behavior—is not historically normative for those who are followers of Christ. The traditions, spiritual resources, and disciplines have never changed—just our perspective of them.

Let's examine some of these traditional tools of faith to see how they can help us respond in love to Jesus Christ.

PRAYER AS A RESPONSE TO LOVE

Prayer is one of the great Christian topics of our day, yet few of us actually engage in it. But prayer can be fulfilling, energizing, and even exciting once it becomes an expression of response to a God we know and trust. When prayer becomes a response to God's initiative, it changes from a narcissistic wrestling match with an adversary to an intimate encounter with someone we cherish. The ancient disciplines of solitude, silence, and listening take on new meaning when we come to Jesus, responding in simple faith.

What does it mean to "respond in simple faith"? In prayer, it means to be willing to place yourself in the hands of God for a time, allowing Him to take you wherever He pleases. Yes, you can arrive with lists, but you must be willing to put them down. Certainly you can come with Scripture and books, formulas and patterns, but you must never hold fast to them. You can close your eyes or look to the heavens—it doesn't really matter, because our God is real, He is with you, and He was listening even before you began to speak.

You don't even have to say anything; you can just be still, together. You can take a walk with your Lord, and know that in your silence there is the depth of prayer. For prayer is found any time you consciously realize that Jesus Christ stands with you, ready to be in communion with you. The key is to step up and focus on Him, as the Scripture calls us to do: "Therefore, holy brothers [and sisters], who share in the heavenly calling, fix your thoughts on Jesus, the apostle and high priest whom we confess" (Hebrews 3:1).

Mother Teresa counsels,

> Love to pray. Feel often during the day the need for prayer, and take trouble to pray. Prayer enlarges the heart until it is capable of containing God's gift of himself. Ask and seek, and your heart will grow big enough to receive him and keep him as your own.[2]

Nike spent millions to plant a simple message in our minds: "Just do it!" That is the way to experience prayer as God intends.

But learning to "love to pray" is easier said than done. This desire can be a frustrating and elusive goal. That is precisely why you need to let go of what you think prayer *ought* to be. Free yourself from expectations and focus on Jesus. God is not so shortsighted as to desire your attention and time and then allow the task to be overwhelming and forbidding. Do you think that God *wants* you to be discouraged and feel like a failure in your prayer life? Blasphemy! He wants to visit, to walk, to laugh, to cry, to listen, to talk. Your prayer is a response to His love for you.

Even Henri Nouwen, who has taught countless believers on prayer and solitude, confesses to struggling at times. He shares with us how he prays during these times:

> Therefore, Lord, I promise I will not run away, not give up, not stop praying, even when it all seems useless, pointless, and a waste of time and effort. I want to let you know that I love you even though I do not feel loved by you, and that I hope in you even though I often experience despair. Let this be a little dying I can do with you and for you as a way of experiencing some solidarity with the millions in this world who suffer far more than I do.[3]

Can you echo this prayer, or something similar? If so, you are on the road to true freedom in your faith.

The more you pray in freedom, the more you will experience freedom in other areas of your faith. Dallas Willard comments,

> Praying with frequency gives us the readiness to pray again as needed from moment to moment. The more we pray, the more we think to pray, and as we see the results of prayer — the responses of our Father to our requests — our confidence in God's power spills over into other areas of our life.[4]

As you approach prayer, there is another important reality to grasp: Prayer not only strengthens us in our quest for a deeper trust in Jesus as our King, it reminds us over and over again that we matter to God. As Eugene Peterson says,

> We live in a noisy world. We are yelled at, promoted, called. Everyone has an urgent message for us. We are surrounded with noise: telephone, radio, television, stereo. Messages are amplified deafeningly. The world is a mob in which everyone is talking at once and no one is willing or able to listen.
>
> But God listens. He not only speaks to us, he listens to us. His listening to us is an even greater marvel than his speaking to us. It is rare to find anyone who listens carefully and thoroughly . . . [where] our minds are taken seriously. When it happens we know that what we say and feel are immensely important. We acquire dignity. We never know how well we think or speak until we find someone who listens to us.[5]

APPRECIATING THE BIBLE

Theological debates rage over the meaning of words, the authenticity of authorship, and the meaning and context of biblical culture. These arguments may have their place in scholarly arenas, but they are far away from life in the pew. Most people who follow Christ believe that the Bible is authoritative and reliable. And although almost every believer would say that the Bible is the most important document of human history, many would also admit that they rarely if ever pick it up and read it.

I do want to acknowledge that many believers spend a great deal of time reading their Bibles. Many of them are involved in regular Bible studies and biblical discipleship programs that teach Scripture. This is good and right and helpful. However, to study the Bible in order to acquire mere academic knowledge of it can be as fruitless as ignoring it altogether. I believe the Bible is not primarily intended to be a valuable document conveying truth. If you want to respond to God's love in your faith in a way that defeats the urge to perform, embrace the Bible as a love letter from a dear Friend who is telling you the deepest secrets of His heart.

Yes, study and teaching are very important. Especially because of the vast distance of years, cultures, and writing styles, the Bible must travel to be properly understood. But study and teaching should be the preparation for seeing God act and hearing God speak through Scripture. Studying the Bible without loving reflection and personal interaction is like preparing for a long trip—fixing the car, getting the maps, making the reservations, buying the traveler's checks—and then never leaving the garage.

The best way I know to appreciate the Bible as a response to God's love is to approach it with the anticipation of time with a long-lost loved one. Jewish theologian Abraham J. Heschel advises:

> To sense the presence of God in the Bible, one must learn *to be present* to God in the Bible. Presence is not a concept, but a situation. To understand love it is not enough to read tales about it. . . . Presence is

not disclosed to those who are unattached and try to judge, to those who have no power to go beyond the values they cherish; to those who sense the story, not the pathos; the idea, not the realness of God.

The Bible is the frontier of the spirit where we must move and live in order to discover and to explore. It is open to him who gives himself to it, who lives with it intimately.[6]

This is the first step in allowing the Bible to draw us deeper into the Kingdom of God: our willingness to be actively involved in whatever passage we happen to be reading, asking God to illuminate the words.

If we deeply desire to find Jesus Christ in Scripture, however, there is another step we must take. This is a second and equally important desire when approaching the Bible: a willingness to act on whatever God brings to our time with Him. It may be a nudge to call someone and apologize, or to stop holding onto a negative feeling that has begun to drag us down, or to make a change in lifestyle. Whatever it is that God whispers as we read and meditate on Scripture will produce one of two results: either we will ignore what we know we are called to be and do—thereby blocking the freedom of following Him by making the Bible seem irrelevant and impotent—or we will open our hearts and respond.

When we fail to do what God asks of us, it is usually because we aren't quite ready to trust Him with the consequences of our actions. We are still holding fast to the ethic of performance. As Robert McGee writes in *The Search For Significance,*

Unfortunately, many of us give only lip-service to the powerful truths of the Scriptures without allowing them to affect the basis of our self-esteem in a radical way. Instead, we continue to seek our security and purpose from worldly sources: personal success, status, beauty, wealth, and the approval of others.

These rewards may fulfill us for a short time, but they soon lead us to a sense of urgency to succeed and be approved again.[7]

If this is how we approach what we read, we will quickly slip back into the performance mentality of living in the kingdom of self. Either we trust the God who loves us or we don't. This in turn means that either we desire to follow Jesus and thereby experience freedom, or we are not yet ready to deny the performance illusion due to our unwillingness to trust God. There are no other options.

This provides for us a kind of litmus test in our quest for a deepening faith and freedom—if the Bible is fresh, new, and exciting, we are most likely seeking what Jesus has for us and are responding accordingly. If we find the Bible to be hard to read, boring, and distant, there may be a block in our walk with God.

Come to the Bible often, lavishly, looking for the joy and freedom God wants to grant you through the reading of His Word.

THE MYSTERY OF WORSHIP

For many of us, the traditional worship service is far from an emotional and heartfelt experience of gratitude for all that God has done. For this we usually blame someone else—either the pastor was boring, or the songs weren't very good, or the announcements were too long, or the kid in the next pew couldn't sit still. It seems like there is always something that makes a typical Sunday morning service feel like a devotional hoop through which God wants us to jump.

But worship can be so much more, as Eugene Peterson suggests:

Familiarity dulls my perceptions. Hurry scatters my attention. Ambition fogs my intelligence. Selfishness restricts my range. Anxiety robs me of appetite. Envy distracts me from what is good and blessed right before me. And then worship brings me to my senses.[8]

Annie Dillard speaks bluntly about what lies at the heart of the privilege of worship:

Worship is dangerous. It is not a retreat from reality, but a direct engagement with ultimate reality: God. Genuine worship is a response to God and what he has done; in it we make ourselves vulnerable to the story of Israel and Jesus. Does anyone have the foggiest idea what sort of power we so blithely invoke? The churches are children playing on the floor with their chemistry sets, mixing up a batch of TNT to kill a Sunday morning. It is madness to wear ladies' straw hats and velvet hats to church; we should all be wearing crash helmets. Ushers should issue life preservers and signal flares; they should lash us to our pews.[9]

Does this sound like your experience? Every time I have read this quote to groups, it has triggered subtle, cynical laughter. Why? After all, worship is the awesome mystery of God and His people coming together in unique and intimate union. It is where we affirm the majesty and passion of God and recognize how all that we are and have is due to His immeasurable love for us. Why, then, is our experience of worship so commonplace, even stagnant? Whose fault is it?

Fault is not the issue. But if it were, it would be mine. When I worship I come to receive. I want good music, I want a flowing program and sharp timing. I want a polished sermon that doesn't ramble on too long. After all, this is my valuable time I'm allotting for worship, isn't it?

But that is precisely the problem: Worship is not *my* time, it is Jesus' time. Every minute of every day He is busy guarding, protecting, leading, loving, and forgiving.

His focused energy is constantly directed at me. Worship is my chance to gaze upon Him. Worship is the small effort I make to assure God that I, too, love Him and am grateful for the relationship that He has provided for me. Whether this worship takes place on a Sunday morning or at noon on Thursday makes no difference to Him. Whenever my heart turns toward Him with gratitude, confession, and praise, I am worshiping. If this is the attitude of my spirit, worship will always be exciting and frightening, humbling and uplifting.

In our culture, corporate worship is the time when the local community of believers gathers as God's family to focus on Jesus Christ. Even if a worship service is boring, self-serving, poorly run, or too long, it can still have a powerful impact on the believer who comes not to receive but to give.

When you go to church, allow yourself to transcend the program and focus on the One who calls you by name. Before it begins, don't chitchat with your friends—silently ask God to honor your heart's desire to thank Him. Do you love Him? Tell Him through your worship. When you join in song, sing to Him. When you give money, whisper a special word of gratitude. When there is a message, listen to what God is saying to you, not what the preacher happens to be talking about. As you do, you will find that no matter what church you attend, the time of corporate worship is a precious, powerful experience.

A QUIET TIME TO STOP AND LISTEN

A quiet time is simply time set apart to be alone with the God who cares. There is no formula that matters, other than what works for you. There are no biblical rules, such as committing a certain amount of time every day in the early morning or before you go to bed. These patterns are simply tools to help you to be disciplined and find what works best for you.

Different seasons require different styles of spending time apart with God. A mother at home with small children cannot be expected to follow the traditional routine of getting up early every day unless she has the stamina to avoid sleep altogether. The college student may have three two-hour blocks in the middle of the day every week. The business person may need to take a half-hour off every other day to be with God. *What* you do and *how* you spend time with Jesus doesn't matter as much as *why* you do it.

The reason for a quiet time is to set aside a given portion of energy to focus on your relationship with God, to hear Him call you by name, to be comforted by His presence. A. W. Tozer urges us,

> It is important that we get still to wait on God. And it is best that we get alone, preferably with our Bible outspread before us. Then if we will we may draw near to God and begin to hear Him speak to us in our hearts. . . . There is no release from our burden apart from the meekness of Christ . . . when we accept ourselves for what we are and cease to pretend.[10]

Although there's no secret to making it work, this time is most valuable when three things are present: prayer (talking to Jesus); meditation (listening to Jesus); and Scripture (learning about Jesus with the Holy Spirit's help).

Meditation is a foreign and often frightening concept for many believers. However, it is not a spooky or fringe method of enjoying and responding to Jesus; it is simply listening to God speak.

If you take time to listen to God, He will speak to you. As hard as this is for people to understand, it is solid biblical teaching:

> Blessed is the man [whose] . . . delight is in the law of the LORD, and on his law he meditates day and night. (Psalm 1:1-2)

I remember the days of long ago; I meditate on all your works and consider what your hands have done. (Psalm 143:5)

Do not let this Book of the Law depart from your mouth; meditate on it day and night, so that you may be careful to do everything written in it. (Joshua 1:8)

The absence of meditation is also a great weakness in the church today. People don't know how to be quiet, to stop, to listen. But this is one of the great gifts God has for us today: to be able to turn off the machines that run our lives and sit quietly, listening to the Voice who reaches out to us over time, space, and circumstance.

I am involved with a group of people in Denver who stop once a month for a half-day silent retreat in community. We have only one goal: to slow down long enough to listen to the Lord as we seek Him. Business leaders, ministers, counselors, homemakers, students—all of us have experienced the value of committing to a few hours a month of silent meditation. To begin learning to respond to Jesus through meditation, a monthly exercise of this type is a good place to start.

SERVICE

"If a true sense of value is to be yours it must come through service." This message, which I pulled out of a fortune cookie at a Chinese restaurant, reflects one of the greatest misunderstandings of the value and benefits of service. Rightly understood, service is nothing more than doing something for someone else. It focuses on the one being served. Whenever our motive is to receive recognition, or even to secretly attain "a true sense of value," then we reduce service to a selfish act that cheaply feigns goodness. In fact, with this distortion, the service itself can stand in the way of allowing Christ to free us, for we remain trapped by the performance illusion.

On the other hand, when we serve with an honest and authentic heart, we will discover one of the most valuable paths to finding freedom in Jesus. The key is our attitude as we approach ministry and service. When we remember who we are in Christ, resting securely on our position as children of the Kingdom, then we have the ability to serve and love without strings attached. Then our service becomes authentic, for in our freedom we become conduits of God's love to others.

When we are moving in the direction of freedom from the need to perform and the need to be acknowledged for what we do, then the discipline of service is an extremely helpful growth tool. As Dallas Willard points out, "Paradoxically perhaps, service is the high road to freedom from bondage to other people."[11]

No matter how busy you are or how stretched you may feel, God has designed you to exercise your freedom by serving others. In fact, freedom can be summarized as *being free to love without selfish motives*. Seeking some avenue of service or ministry is an important affirmation of and step toward growth, for in the discipline of service we will experience a richness of Kingdom living that can be found nowhere else.

This type of sacrificial commitment to selfless service becomes even more essential as we take on greater degrees of leadership or authority. It will help keep us involved in real-life issues and guard against our seduction by the false allure of the performance ethic. Dallas Willard summarizes it best:

> I believe the discipline of service is even more important for Christians who find themselves in positions of influence, power, and leadership. . . . Those who would live this pattern must attain it through the discipline of service in the power of God, for that alone will train them to exercise great power without corrupting their souls.[12]

CONCLUSION

All too easily, our practice of any of these traditional disciplines and norms of the Christian faith can slip into a performance mode. We must strive never to confuse these disciplines of commitment with the need to perform—for God, for those in spiritual authority, or for anyone else.

However, without such disciplines and a group of people who share these convictions walking through them with us, most of us will simply not pursue our first love, no matter how badly we want to. This kind of discipline just doesn't come naturally to most of us.

Beloved of God, go after Jesus Christ and His Kingdom with abandonment and a reckless discipline. But don't ever forget that you need never *earn* approval from God or people. You are precious in God's eyes as you are. If you choose to relax in your pursuit of Jesus, the cost will be great. You can never hope to be free from the performance illusion unless you set your heart and mind on His Kingdom. His love is what draws you to desire Him, and the disciplines are the wings upon which you may travel to your first love.

13

RESPONDING TO GOD'S LOVE IN MY FAMILY

When I get honest, I admit I am a bundle of paradoxes.
I believe and I doubt, I hope and get discouraged,
I love and I hate, I feel bad about feeling good, I feel guilty
about not feeling guilty.
I am trusting and suspicious. I am honest and I still play
games. Aristotle said I am a rational animal;
I say I am an angel with an incredible capacity for beer.
To live by grace means to acknowledge my whole life story,
the light side and the dark. In admitting my shadow side
I learn who I am and what God's grace means.
As Thomas Merton put it, "A saint is not someone who is
good but who experiences the goodness of God."

BRENNAN MANNING
The Ragamuffin Gospel

The family is the one place where we cannot hide, we cannot run, we cannot pretend. If we choose to live from the center of our convictions by responding to the love that God has for us instead of trying to earn our place, the most crucial laboratory in our lives is our family.

In chapter 2, we saw that as hard as parents may try, parental love alone can never fully meet a child's need for unconditional love and acceptance. That raises the question, Even if we do want to live differently in our family, what would be different? What do we have to offer our loved ones?

We can bring to our children, spouses, siblings, and parents a commitment to point them, relationally, to the source of healing and unconditional love. Here is where grace can make the biggest difference, for God has a way of using fragile, sinful, broken people who have come to Him with gratitude to touch the lives of others. God's message of gentleness and kindness toward us is not limited to inner whispers of the Spirit. It can be transmitted in a parent's hug, in the listening ear of a brother or sister, or in the tender support of a stepparent. God asks us simply to be a vessel through which He can move.

In this chapter, we will be looking at what it takes to be in relationship with our children and our spouse as a response to God's love in the context of family.

LOVING YOUR CHILDREN

I believe it is a parent's task to "train a child in the way he should go" in hopes of fulfilling the biblical consequence, "and when he is old he will not turn from it" (Proverbs 22:6). This oft-quoted passage, however, has been wielded as a weapon of guilt as often as it has been cited as an encouragement to love. Many parents have fought to hold tightly to this verse, claiming it as a promise of God, only to see their children externally rebel from the faith.

A rigid misunderstanding of this verse often feeds a performance theology. Consequently, far too many parents wander from the faith—beaten, discouraged, and disillusioned. They think they have been abandoned by the Lord. It is not the Lord who has failed them, however, but the teaching they have received.

This verse brings two great and timeless truths to us, but neither is presented in the form of a "promise of God" that can somehow be claimed by the zealous, performing believer. The first truth is grounded in the nature of wisdom literature. The Proverbs is a compilation of God-given wisdom for living, with sound advice on the causes and effects of wise decisions and choices. But careful study (which we don't have room to detail here) reveals that many of the consequences mentioned in Proverbs are dependent not only on the person attempting to live a godly lifestyle, but also on the choices of the recipient—in this case, the child being raised. Parents, in other words, are not totally responsible for how their children will ultimately choose to live: their children are! But, all things being equal, parents who attempt to train their child in the ways of unconditional love and grace will have a good shot at seeing their children take hold of this way of life.

A second timeless truth in this passage is that despite how children may choose to live, the parents who were committed to loving them for who they were and not for what they did will have given them this powerful message: "We love *you*. Not because of what you have done or said, or whether you have chosen our lifestyle, but because you are our precious child." This is not dependent upon the response of the child, and no lifestyle choice will ever be strong enough to wipe away such a powerful message of love.

I'd like to suggest three key ingredients that enable us to respond to God's love and grace with our children: *affirmation*, *support*, and *friendship*.

Affirmation
Earl Palmer distinguishes between affirmation and unconditional love in his discussion of the Apostle Paul's boldness with his accomplishments to the Corinthians:

> I believe that the desire for admiration, for the kind of respect that comes from a task well done, is a sign of spiritual and emotional health. . . . Though Paul apologizes to the Corinthians for his overwhelming directness, that apology does not negate the basic healthiness of Paul's approach to the human need for recognition. . . . But what is of vital importance for us is to note that Paul does not confuse admiration for love.[1]

Affirmation that shows us we are in the right spot and living according to our God-given gifts and talents is good and healthy. But the conviction that we are loved for who we are is vastly different, and goes far deeper.

The difference between these two is the clear boundary between love and critical assessment and evaluation. The first provides an atmosphere in which children know they are loved and accepted absolutely, unconditionally, as they are at the present moment—warts and all. The second provides feedback, both positive affirmation and constructive help, based on performance, actions, ability, and effort. Once children are convinced they are loved as they are, they will be much better able to hear praise without gloating and receive criticism without defensiveness.

Affirmation tied to performance is a gift when, and only when, children don't need it for basic approval. This is often a hard line to walk, but making this distinction is one of the greatest gifts you can give your child.

Support
All children fail. It might be in arguing too much, wetting their pants, stealing something, cheating in school, or lying to you. What do you do when your child fails you, or hurts you, or lets you down? What does it mean to be free as one loved by God, not performing in your relationship with your family, but loving without reservation, when everything inside you wants to get angry, lash out, and give up? How do you support your kids when they fail?

First, recognize it is rarely easy. Some situations may even require extreme solutions. But one foundational principle centers at the heart of God, and it comes from the lips of Jesus: "My command is this: Love each other as I have loved you" (John 15:12). Supporting your children means recognizing that you have failed at least as much as they have. Therefore, you need lovingly to grant them room to fail, and be there to pick them up and dust them off when their failure inevitably occurs. Even though love demands that behavior have consequences—what some call discipline—you must convince them that their failure will never affect your love for them.

The minimal guarantee we must make to people is that they will be loved—always, under every circumstance, with no exception. The second guarantee is that they will be totally accepted, without reservation. The third thing we must guarantee people is that no matter how miserably they fail or how blatantly they sin, unreserved forgiveness is theirs for the asking with no bitter taste left in anyone's mouth.[2]

This kind of spirit is what God calls us to as parents. Some may protest that this viewpoint glosses over sin without regard for how behavior and failure can hurt others. Shouldn't there be consequences to failure and rebellion? Yes, certainly; but that does not deny the truth of the call to love. Loving our children doesn't mean letting their behavior go unchecked, for discipline is love in action. Even the Lord disciplines: "Those whom I love I rebuke and discipline" (Revelation 3:19).

There may be times when we need to impose or allow drastic consequences for a child's behavior and choices. But all discipline must be undergirded with great compassion, tenderness, and mercy, for the goal remains love, even in the midst of consequences.

Friendship

All children, regardless of age, want to be their parents' friend. When our oldest was a year old, Dee and I heard a sermon about making friends with your kids. We were so deeply touched that we made a commitment right then and there to build authentic, trusting, and loving friendships with each of our children.

This commitment has grown into a philosophy of life rather than a list of duties, for friendship is too spontaneous, too dynamic to be confined by legalistic rules of performance. We don't require our kids to spend time with us, for example, but we do all we can to encourage it. We go out for family dinners a couple of times a month. Dee and I plan one-on-one dates with each of our kids, letting them set the agenda, asking them to initiate the topics of conversation, asking the kinds of questions that prove we care about their life. When I travel to speak to a group, especially to a youth convention or conference, I usually take one or more of my kids, and ask them to help me plan my talks, pray with me, and critique me afterward.

To befriend your children means to seek them out—not with your agenda, but with theirs. (For example, I can't stand going to Chuck E. Cheese's pizza and game parlor, but they love it!) It means asking good questions about their hopes, fears, dreams, friendships, school, and plans. It means giving up reading the paper during family breakfast, or having family dinner as often as possible *without* the television on in the background. Building a friendship tells your kids that you value them as people, and there is no greater love you can show them.

LOVING YOUR SPOUSE

In recent years, Dee and I have been on a campaign to bring wholeness, joy, and health to marriages. Sometimes it feels as if we're in a losing battle, because it seems that every force in our culture is bent on destroying what's left of the institution of marriage.

A *USA Today*-sponsored survey on marriage included several questions about unfaithfulness in marriage.[3] Here is a typical question:

> If you've never had an affair, why not?
> a. satisfied with my spouse
> b. fear of being caught
> c. no opportunity
> d. other.

The questions offered no possible response about commitment, or having made a promise to my spouse, or to society, or to God. Apparently, the only options in the United States for not having an affair are either selfish satisfaction at the present time, or fear, or lack of a chance (but presumably still looking).

The *Seattle Post Intelligencer* reported that a couple in England was denied the right to adopt a child because of "too happy a marriage"; they would not be able to expose a youngster to enough "negative experiences." The authorities explained: "It would seem from the interviews and reports that both of you have had few, if any, negative experiences when children yourselves, and also seem to enjoy a marital relationship where rows and arguments have no place."[4] Thus they were barred from adopting a child; their life was too out of sync with the rest of the world in its happiness and stability because of a healthy marriage.

Even in this selfish, broken, and destructive mess of American marriages, the gospel has the power to change things for those who are willing to respond to the love of God in their marriages. There are many vital ingredients to a successful marriage, but I'd like to suggest four proven ways to build a heathy, growing marital relationship.

Submit to Each Other

I have always found it interesting to note where scholarly translators of our Bibles choose to make paragraph and subtitle divisions. Any student of Scripture can tell you that in the original languages there are no such divisions; there isn't even punctuation as we know it. Any time you see a subtitle or paragraph in your English Bible, it's the result of a decision of a group of learned editors and scholars. The biggest goof, in my humble opinion, lies at the heart of the marriage relationship. It is found in Ephesians 5, beginning with verse 21.

For example, the *New International Version* has followed standard tradition in this case by inserting a paragraph and subtitle break between verse 21, "Submit to one another out of reverence for Christ," and verse 22, "Wives, submit to your husbands as to the Lord." Time and again ministers, writers, and public speakers will begin any discussion of marriage at verse 22, under the mistaken perception that "this is how the Bible starts the discussion." But that is not true. It is how the International Bible Society chose to order it.

I have a different view. As I have studied the Bible concerning marriage duties and roles, I've concluded that Paul had finished one train of thought in verse 20 and was laying the foundation upon which marriage rests in verse 21. I believe that, yes, there are distinctive scriptural responsibilities for husbands and wives, but they must be understood as secondary to the basic injunction of mutual submission "out of reverence for Christ."

This means that I must uphold a mutual and lifelong commitment to value my marriage partner as an equal partner before the Lord. It means that neither husband nor wife has any right to make decisions without consulting and listening to the other. Practically, it might mean that a husband discusses his golf schedule with his wife as often as she consults him about scheduling her night out with friends.

A very tangible step in responding to God's love is to be willing to lay down my rights and privileges for the rights and privileges of my spouse. This is difficult at times, and may occasionally require a few hard swallows of pride, but it's what it means to love your partner as Jesus has loved you.

Be Honest with Each Other
There is no doubt that especially in marriage, believers must "be kind and compassionate to one another, forgiving each other, just as in Christ God forgave you" (Ephesians 4:32). But just before this command, Paul had exhorted that "each of you must put off falsehood and speak truthfully to his neighbor, for we are all members of one body" (4:25). The balance between these two is "speaking the truth in love" (4:15).

Confrontation is one kind of honesty. Another kind is keeping open accounts—a day-to-day kind of honesty that involves the little things as much as the big things.

The first sign of cancer in a marriage covenant is the secret decision to choose autonomy. It may begin with something as innocent as a small purchase, or allowing seductive but "harmless" thoughts to get a foothold. But once the seed of deceit is planted, it quickly grows into a thornbush of hiding, deception, and mistrust. Soon the marriage is cluttered with superficial issues that never really get to the heart of the problem. Most often when a marriage dissolves the cause is simple: somebody (many times both people) made the decision to hide.

Dee and I have attempted to fend off this process by committing ourselves to total and complete honesty. However, that is far easier said than done. She may want to buy something she knows will cause a rift, or I may schedule a speaking engagement I want to accept but know will adversely affect her. Eventually, however, it all comes out anyway, and it's so much easier if we keep short accounts with each other. There can be incredible bondage in hiding, but great (and sometimes humbling and even difficult) freedom in openness and honesty.

Support Each Other's Dreams

Before I met Dee, I learned a great deal from two older friends about marriage. One enjoyed the happiest and most fulfilling marriage I have ever seen, and the other was divorced. They both shared the same message with me: to truly love my wife, I needed to make her plans, dreams, callings, and desires as important as mine.

This was revolutionary teaching to me, because I had always thought that the man was the "spiritual leader" of the home, and therefore his decisions were the ones that mattered. I even went to a prominent seminar on family conflicts depicting the husband as a hammer, the wife as a chisel, and the children as diamonds to be shaped. This image was part of God's supposed "Chain of Command," but it is easy to see how someone could interpret the husband's job as hitting his wife over the head with his leadership!

Despite teachings such as these, I became convinced that the advice my two friends had given to me was truly God's heart for marriage. Marriage is the commitment of two people walking through life *together*, each willing to do whatever it takes to help the other succeed in his or her life's calling. When I met Dee, she had come to the same conclusions about marriage, and so from day one we have been on the same page.

My most important task in life, therefore, is to present my wife to Jesus Christ as a woman who has been given every chance to be all that God has called her to be. She, likewise, is committed to my growth and desires. When these tasks conflict—which, because of our desire to submit to one another, is very rare—we prayerfully sit and talk, working out solutions and, if necessary, compromises, seeking God's best throughout the process.

For example, a few years ago I was invited to go to Russia (the USSR at the time) on a training mission with Young Life for three weeks. Dee encouraged me to go, though we both knew that it would be hard on her and the kids. The night I got back, she informed me that she had decided that she wanted to go back to school and pursue a Master's degree in counseling. Our kids were growing up, and she had sacrificed for my ministry, writing, traveling, speaking, and teaching, and there were things she felt that God was calling her to do, too. It took some careful planning and renegotiation of roles and expectations, especially so our kids would not be adversely affected. Today, Dee is about to complete her degree. It has been a joy to walk together in this, knowing that all that Dee and I have accomplished, we have done together. And our marriage is better for it.

Listen to and Communicate with Each Other

Dee and I believe that the greatest strength in our ministry with each other and with couples is our ability to communicate and to listen to each other. We are now leading workshops in marriage communication, and have published a book helping couples learn from what has helped us (*Let*

Me Ask You This: Conversations That Draw Couples Closer, NavPress, 1991). In this communication tool and devotional for couples we have a section entitled "Groundrules for Communication." The basic principles are as follows:

1. Beware of interrupting each other.
2. Beware the temptation for one person to dominate.
3. Use word pictures to describe feelings that are hard to communicate.
4. When an issue begins to divide you, one person must take on the role of the objective narrator.
5. Feelings are neutral, and therefore it does no good to try to argue them away.
6. When sharing, do all you can not to attack your spouse.
7. When you hit a crossroads, don't allow a new thought until you have repeated what you have said so far.
8. It takes time to talk.

CONCLUSION

When we are committed to this type of love with our children and our spouse, we will give them a glimpse of what it means to be loved by God. And we will also find that they are more willing to love us in this same way.

However, what we receive in return cannot be our motive, for the only real ability we have to love our family at all comes from the knowledge that God has first loved us. But when we love others for who they are, they can begin to see themselves as valuable, which frees them from their need to perform in an attempt to find love, acceptance, and forgiveness. This is what it means to respond to the love of God in our families: to love as we have been loved.

14

RESPONDING TO GOD'S LOVE IN MY FRIENDSHIPS

Relatively few of us experience the blend of contentment and godly intensity that God desires for each person. From life's outset, we find ourselves on the prowl, searching to satisfy some inner, unexplained yearning. Our hunger causes us to search for people who will love us. Our desire for acceptance pressures us to perform for the praise of others.

ROBERT S. McGEE, *The Search for Significance*

Every time you meet another human being you have the opportunity. It's a chance at holiness. For you will do one of two things, then. Either you will build him up or you will tear him down.

WALTER WANGERIN
Ragman and Other Cries of Faith

I believe that McGee's assertion that we "search for people who will love us" is true, even for those who have willingly chosen to live their life in the Kingdom of God, striving to let go of the need to perform. We have been built with an innate desire and need for relationships, for depth of friendship—and not just from God. True, the Lord is the source of our security and the anchor we hold fast to as we go through life, but the tangible, touchable goodness and grace of God is also experienced through trusted relationships. God has built us to want and need friends.

There are two types of friends: those who make us feel the need to perform for their approval, and those who free us to be ourselves. Wangerin says we are either built up or torn down by every person we meet; there is no in-between. At first glance this may be an overstatement. However, as I consider those I have known over the years, they tend to fall into one of two camps—either I feel cared for and supported by their friendship, or I find myself nervous and on guard whenever I encounter them.

We all share a need for authentic and safe friendships with people who can help to free us from the need to perform. But few of us take the time to find such friends.

Friendships can be generally categorized in three groups: acquaintances, friends, and soul mates. Acquaintances are those people to whom we are called to give freely of ourselves. They may be strangers, coworkers, or neighbors. We may know them externally, but our hearts are not connected, and because we live as the beloved children of the King we don't need them. Our call to them is to give when we can, to listen, to love, to accept—in short, to be avenues by which the power of unconditional acceptance flows to them, no strings attached.

In the second category, our relationships tend to be more a mutual give and take. We may try to live as though our friends can't hurt us or drag us down, but by definition our lives are connected, and therefore we are vulnerable. We are still called to give, but we also look to them to reinforce our need for genuine acceptance. Sometimes we receive it from these people, and sometimes we are pulled away. This is why there must be another category for us to explore in our move away from the performance ethic.

To experience wholeness in the Kingdom of God we must have relationships among all three groups, for the first two are filled with the kind of people who draw us away from Christ's acceptance of us into the world of performance. Only those we deeply trust as soul mates can help us to flesh out our response to God's love in the everyday.

Soul mates are friends we can trust with our every thought. We can trust them with the deepest and darkest secrets of our hearts, and know they will still accept us. Each of us needs soul mates, and we must give top priority to developing and cultivating such relationships. When there are people around us who purposefully remind us that our identity is rooted in authenticity and legitimacy before God, we can shed the vestiges of the performance illusion.

QUALITIES OF A SOUL MATE

Six qualities mark a soul mate. Although they may not all be present at the same time and in the same season, they are goals we can strive for with those special few to whom God has called us. Most important is our willingness to care for each other in the following ways.

Mutual Commitment

The most vital aspect of this list of qualities is *a mutual commitment of love and trust*. It is not possible to be a soul mate with someone who chooses not to walk through life with you in the same way. You will be continually forced to perform for that person in order to maintain the closeness you desire. There are friends you have who, given the chance, would be very open to making a substantial commitment of depth of friendship. Start slowly, but be sure to seek mutuality as the relationship deepens, or you may be headed for disappointment and struggle.

Regular Time Together

The *amount* of time need not be a major issue in strengthening a soul mate relationship, for soul mates may have vastly different schedules, responsibilities, and even geographic locations. But a willingness to commit to regular, uninterrupted, and focused time together is essential. Without regular opportunities to hear from each, to confess and struggle together about the complex nature of living in this broken world, it is far too easy to hide from each other.

Openness and Honesty

In his profound book *Primacy of the Heart*, Henri Nouwen made this observation:

Why do we keep hiding our deepest feelings from each other? We suffer much, but we also have great gifts of healing for each other. By hiding our pain, we also hide our ability to heal. Even in such a loving and caring community as this of L'Arche, there is more suffering than necessary, more loneliness than necessary. We are called to confess to each other and forgive each other, and thus discover the abundant mercy of God. But at the same time, we are so terribly afraid that we may be wounded even more deeply. This fear keeps us prisoners, even when the prison has no walls! How radical Jesus' message of love is! How difficult! And how necessary![1]

In chapter 6, we looked at the tragic loneliness of people in our culture. I think it's safe to say that many people in our culture, perhaps even most, don't have the slightest clue regarding what it means to be honest in a relationship—or with themselves, for that matter. And yet we are all yearning for someone to come alongside us, who knows all about us, and is willing to love us anyway. This is the essence of love in the Kingdom of God.

God obviously knows all there is to know about us, and it still doesn't change anything: He loves us as we are. To help us grow in this understanding and live as free men and women, we are greatly boosted by people who love us in this same way. We need it and long for it. Yet we run from it.

If you honestly desire to flee the performance illusion, it is essential that you have one friend or more with whom you can be completely candid. Whether it is a secret fear, a desire to cry, a struggle with lust, or even a contemplation of adultery, the most powerful way to diffuse potential sin is to throw it into the light of openness, honesty, and confession. It is simply too easy to talk ourselves into the worst possible decision when we are hiding in the darkness of the kingdom of self.

Find a friend and take the gamble to share openly. It

may be painful, but the consequences of not being honest will be far worse down the road. God never intended for us to hide from each other. He knows our weakness and propensity for allowing sin to bring us happiness and value. Don't let the darkness gain a foothold. Tell your soul mate everything.

Encouragement

A soul mate's task in loving as Jesus loves is to remind you over and over again that you are unique, wonderful, and gifted just as you are — not to make sure that you know what all your failures are. There is a balance here, and we will get to that, but it does not diminish the fact that we need a few fans in our corner, cheering us on.

Encouragement does not necessarily mean 100 percent affirmation for everything you do or accomplish; it's much deeper than that. Encouragement is the fundamental belief that you are valuable, that you have worth. It is more the quality that says, "I believe in you, no matter what you do." A soul mate is an encourager.

Confrontation

A major turning point in my life came from a totally unexpected source. Donn was a young, new staff member in my Young Life area, and I was responsible for supervising him. During his first year, he was meek, mild, almost shy, and very teachable. We would meet weekly, and as we spent more time together, I grew to greatly appreciate Donn's heart, gifts, and abilities. Donn seemed to soak up all that I could throw at him, and he never appeared to mind when I asked him to take on new tasks. He was easy to like.

In the spring, we ran a weekend camp with over six hundred high school kids crammed into Forest Home Conference Center outside Los Angeles. I nearly always had my hand in the program and leadership during those years, and that weekend I took to task another leader over some aspect of the program. Afterward I forgot about it instantly, but Donn didn't.

The next Tuesday during our weekly meeting, Donn said, "I have to talk to you about something."

Sensing his anxiety, I simply said, "Okay, shoot."

"Do you realize how you treated Dave Saturday?"

"No, not really."

"Well I do, and he was devastated! Chap, you don't even know how much you walk over people when you have a task to accomplish. Quality is important, and I respect you for your commitment to kids, but we need to figure out how to keep you from destroying people in the process."

I was stunned. Not hurt, exactly—just taken aback. No one close to me, other than my wife, had ever so openly and honestly confronted me. But because I knew how much Donn appreciated and loved me, I was able not only to listen but to seek his help. I'm pretty sure that at that time of my life I would have responded with bitter defensiveness to anyone else who spoke to me like that. But Donn had won the right to be heard by me. If he had kept quiet, I might never have known how I was railroading people in the name of ministry. That day Donn became a soul mate, beginning a journey of growth that continues to this day.

I have a few friends I am afraid to confront for fear of how they would take it. But if I am unwilling to stand alongside of them, helping to convince them of their value even while I am telling them my concern, I am no soul mate. Soul mates take risks trying to help the person they love to grow through criticism.

Usually, a soul mate is a great question-asker before being an advice-giver. In order to point out to others where they need to grow, two things must be securely in place: a solid, growing trust in the friendship, and a willingness to get all the facts first. Asking questions provides both these safeguards. But true soul mates will confront when it is necessary, because they will not allow a blind spot to keep a friend from being all that God has called him or her to be.

Sacrificial

Finally, a soul mate can freely say, "I promise to be there for you whenever and wherever you need me." This must always be tempered by the other primary relationships in our lives, children and spouses. But unless being sacrificially available would cause great harm to those primary relationships, as soul mates we must be committed to dropping all else in the time of need.

Recently, a good friend of mine went through a political and very tough job displacement. Through it all there was a group of five or six families constantly on the phone, even on airplanes, trying to shore up the brokenness surrounding this family. From the world's perspective the circumstances surrounding this departure would have been devastating. However, this family not only survived the ordeal, but God allowed them to come out of it with their heads held high, knowing their lives were in Jesus' hands, and that God still valued them, despite all that had happened. The soul mates who rallied around this man and his family showed to the world the value of commitment to relationships that are based not on performance but on acceptance and genuine love.

CONCLUSION

Do you have any soul mates? If you do, thank God for the gift of these friends; go through this list and see how you are fulfilling each other's needs of love. If you don't, there is no time like the present to begin to cultivate a friend or two.

When God called you out of the kingdom of self into the Kingdom of God, He also called you to a depth of friendship those caught up in the performance illusion cannot know, for they can't slow down long enough to find true friendship. As you take those steps that will help you to live in freedom from the need to perform, you can help your friends. *You* can be the first step in someone else's journey away from the need to perform, just by being the kind of friend who loves not because of how that person performs or looks, but because he or she is a valuable gift to all of us.

This is what it means to respond to God's love in your friendships. Take a few long lunches, make some phone calls, and begin building what really matters: friendships that bring meaning to life.

15

RESPONDING TO GOD'S LOVE IN THE TASKS OF LIFE

I'm scared to death every time I get up to pitch.

MAJOR-LEAGUE PITCHER DENNIS ECKERSLEY

The pressure on a professional athlete in our culture may be far beyond what most of us could ever understand—at least on the surface. But the internal pressure to perform is relative. A basketball player who can ignore a noisy, arm-waving crowd and sink a free throw may crumble emotionally under the torment of divorce. For every one of us, there are pressures we can handle easily and those that drive us to the brink.

But when Dennis Eckersley, award-winning ace reliever for the Oakland Athletics, admitted in a TV interview how frightened he was whenever he approached the mound, he was talking about a deeper pressure. It wasn't just the crowd, although that was part of it. It wasn't even the individual batters he had to face. The pressure he felt ultimately came down to the question, "Do I still have it?" or even, "Did I *ever* have it?" With this fear constantly gnawing at his self-confidence, Dennis Eckersley has gone to the mound game after game and once again proven that he indeed "has it." But this truth hasn't erased his fear or his pressure to perform.

Most of us would agree that the struggle to succeed in the marketplace is one of the greatest daily pressures we face. For some it may be an inner drive for excellence (at least on the surface); for others latent insecurity and the need for attention and accolades; for still others the pressure of financial issues. These three interrelated areas all have the power to steal away our freedom to live out of response to the love of God. Let's look at how our freedom in Christ affects the pressures we all feel in our everyday tasks.

THE DRIVE TO ACHIEVE

The inner drive to become the best, to make the most of life, to advance over the competition, is so ingrained in some of us that it seems as natural as breathing. One friend told me that there is a certain temperament, a "killer instinct," that is necessary to survive in much of the modern American corporate world. Anyone who has tried to feed a family on commission would be the first to tell you that without such a drive to be the very best, you have little hope of even surviving.

Some people seem to thrive in competitive, even dangerous, climates. What does it mean for someone like this to be free to respond to the love of God?

We have already explored the various reasons behind our cultural need to perform. Since we have all been affected, at least to some degree, we are all in need of someone to rescue us—even those of us whose drive springs as much from personal temperament as from cultural pressures.

This does *not* mean, however, that we must be freed from our personalities. Family background, lifestyle choices, and other events and people have all helped to mold us as a person—yet ultimately, God is the Master Weaver of our personality. When we come to Him out of gratitude and love, seeking to follow Him as one set free, He does not ask us to become someone else. *He* will do all the changing, from the inside. All He asks of us is to place our drive and ambition at His feet and remain in intimate friendship with Him.

If you are driven to succeed, then, your task is straightforward. Your call is to take what you know of yourself and freely relinquish it to Christ, anticipating His presence in and through your personality. Many of the greatest heroes of the faith have been driven by the desire to succeed, and they needed to learn how to place their personalities under the lordship of Christ.

The Apostle Paul, for example, was extremely rigid and driven. But Jesus intercepted Paul (Saul, at the time) in the middle of his zealous campaign to destroy the early believers, and Paul became a changed man. It was not Paul's personality that changed, however; it was Paul's priorities, compassion, and heart. Paul became a man who was driven by the desire to do good, rather than by the desire to wreak vengeance. A religious zealot for God became a passionate friend of God. Paul remained driven, but his drive was redirected by the love of God in Christ Jesus.

If you are naturally and freely a driven and success-oriented person, this is a gift from God. It is not, however, a gift without cost. The greatest challenge you will face is giving your drive for earthly, financial, and corporate success over to the One who has loved you. The faith experience for you is learning what it means to harness your drive in such a way that God will be able to build the kind of character within you that you were created to have.

If you are highly motivated to achieve, the temptation will be great to succeed because of what achievement does *for you*, instead of how God is using you to influence and serve others. You may even feel that the good you accomplish is solely *because of* you, instead of due to the grace you have received. To live as one set free from the need to perform is to respond to God's love by allowing your personality, temperament, and energy to become His tools.

THE FEAR OF FAILURE

Not everyone has such a strong, innate desire to be successful. Many people simply want to be noticed and appreciated
for what they have to offer. But the longer we remain capti-
vated by the performance illusion, the deeper we stuff our
need to be noticed, replacing it with the need to perform.

This is where I have lived for many years—trying to
convince others that I am gifted and worthy of accolades,
while *really* wanting someone to say that I was valuable.
The most tangible problem I have faced in this struggle
has been the fear of failure. When I am performing, I feel
that there is no room for failure. As I seek to be free from
my *need* to be good at whatever I attempt, I find myself
still trying to fulfill the inner drive that says, "*This* will
prove that you are valuable, after all." I am in a no-win
situation, trapped between two lies—the lie that says my
performance can bring me the attention I need, and the lie
that I will be able to perform well enough to meet these
needs.

Many performers are stifled by the nagging fear that
whispers, "Who am I kidding that I can do this?" No amount
of accomplishment can silence the inner message that they
are inadequate to the tasks they face. The pastor who has
preached hundreds of times still gets caught up in the "Well,
how did I do?" syndrome. The salesperson who has always
surpassed quota still gets up at five to "get a jump on the
competition," though the exhaustion seems to never let up.
The graduate student who has maintained a 3.8 grade point
average still gets angry over a "B." These are all symptoms of
the performance ethic: "I am what I do, and so I had better be
great; anything less, and I am nothing."

Fear of failure presents a real challenge for the person
who would like to defeat the need to perform but continually hears voices telling her that she doesn't measure up.
As Henri Nouwen says, "How do we get in touch with
our chosenness [by our Lord] when we are surrounded

by rejections?"[1] He goes on to formulate three guidelines for the performer who wishes to be freed:

First of all, you have to keep unmasking the world about you for what it is: manipulative, controlling, power-hungry and, in the long run, destructive. The world tells you many lies about who you are, and you simply have to be realistic enough to remind yourself of this. . . .

Secondly, you have to keep looking for people and places where your truth is spoken and where you are reminded of your deepest identity as the chosen one. Yes, we must dare to opt consciously for our chosenness and not allow our emotions, feelings or passions to seduce us into self-rejection. . . .

Thirdly, you have to celebrate your chosenness constantly. This means saying "thank you" to God for having chosen you, and "thank you" to all who remind you of your chosenness. Gratitude is the most fruitful way of deepening your consciousness that you are not an "accident," but a divine choice.[2]

What Nouwen asserts may seem obvious on the surface, but few actually go after those proactively. I have noticed that my moments of greatest victory over my insecurities and my need to perform have occurred when I have employed one or all of these strategies. To remind myself of the never-ending lies of the world, to gather around me soul mates who care, and to live out of gratitude for who I am in Christ—this is the road to freedom for the performer, especially one caught in the trap of low self-esteem.

THE PRESSURE OF MONEY

With the pressure to succeed from every corner—growing up in our educational system, parental encouragement for achievement, constant media reminders of how much we lack and how far we have to go—there remains perhaps the largest and most potent voice demanding constant performance: money.

A friend and I were discussing our financial woes recently. He is a highly successful and well-paid executive. I am—well, a seminary professor who has written a few books and speaks occasionally (doing fine, thank you). As he went on and on lamenting the precariousness of his situation, he suddenly stopped and said, "How do people make it on thirty-two thousand a year? That's the average, you know. How do they survive?"

I wanted to tell him, "It's not easy . . ." but that wasn't his point. He was realizing that with all of his resources and opportunities, he still felt trapped by the need to perform even more in order to remain on the precarious lifestyle precipice he had climbed. He was also realizing that he had it much better than the majority in our culture.

As we talked, we both came to comprehend this one simple truth: Under the influence of our culture's push to achieve, we are always looking for the next new adventure—to buy a better car, to take that vacation, to attend the next movie, to go to the big ball game. It takes money to live this way. And it usually takes *more* money than we have. Thus we are compelled by our desire to have more, our hearts are restless, and we continue searching for that next purchase that will satisfy.

To respond to the love of God in the midst of financial pressures and priorities is to see money for what it *is* and what it is *not*. Money *is* powerful in its ability to seduce us, but it is *not* the means to happiness, fulfillment, or security. Money is necessary for living, useful for doing good and helping others, and a gift of God. But we must also recognize that it is a serious threat to finding freedom in Christ's love.

Money itself is neither good nor bad. As you seek to be free from the pressure of financial struggle, learn to view money not as an enemy but as a tool through which God can prove His love and care. Don't be afraid of money, but beware of letting it control you. God is concerned about your heart; how you handle money is a reflection of what is in your heart. God will give you all you need — and often far more than you need. When it comes to your money, do you trust God enough to respond out of love for Him? This is what matters to our Lord.

THE PREOCCUPATION WITH WORRY

Aside from money, the chief vocation of many in our culture is a preoccupation with worry. Worry about will happen, worry about what won't happen, worry about what will happen if something else doesn't happen. We worry about money, jobs, politics, the stock market, our church, our friends, our marriage, our kids, and our faith. We worry about whether we worry too much, and then we worry that we don't seem to care enough.

Worry is not only annoying, it is paralyzing. It keeps us from moving through life in simple faith. Worry keeps us from risk, and without risk, there is no freedom in living. Worry is one of the greatest enemies to walking in the Kingdom of God, because it is the antithesis of trust. Oswald Chambers observed that "fretting springs from a determination to get our own way."[3] The psalmist warned that worry "leads only to evil" (Psalm 37:8). Jesus Himself spoke to the pointlessness of worrying:

> "Therefore I tell you, do not worry about your life,
> what you will eat or drink; or about your body, what
> you will wear. Is not life more important than food,
> and the body more important than clothes? Look at
> the birds of the air; they do not sow or reap or store
> away in barns, and yet your heavenly Father feeds
> them. Are you not much more valuable than they?
> Who of you by worrying can add a single hour to his
> life? . . .

"So do not worry, saying, 'What shall we eat?'
or 'What shall we drink?' or 'What shall we wear?'
For the pagans run after all these things, and your
heavenly Father knows that you need them. But seek
first his kingdom and his righteousness, and all these
things will be given to you as well. Therefore do
not worry about tomorrow, for tomorrow will worry
about itself. Each day has enough trouble of its own."
(Matthew 6:25-27,31-34)

"Naive!" you cry. But is it really such a leap to trust that
if God does exist, and His character is trustworthy, and He
counts me as precious to Him, that He is able to handle the
absolute essentials of life without my having to lose sleep?

Once again, the formula is straightforward, almost
insultingly so. Either we believe Jesus or we don't. Fretting
and worrying produce only negative results. Absolutely
nothing can be gained from them. If we choose to live
according to the performance ethic, then we have good
cause to worry, because we're on our own. But when we
decide to respond to Jesus' love for us by forcing ourselves
to step back and get His perspective, learning how to trust
Him with the practical things in life, then we can truly rest.
We are free to risk, to move, to experiment, because we know
the One to whom we belong.

As in the drive to achieve, the fear of failure, and the
striving for material success, every situation and circumstance in life comes down to this basic question — to whom
do I belong? If I truly believe the gospel, that Jesus Christ has
called me by name, then responding in faith to the incredible love God has for me will make every issue clear, with
the solution to all of life's struggles within my grasp.

16

CARRYING ON THE FIGHT OF FREEDOM

The little girl was barely five, and she could not understand why Daddy was gone. The divorce was difficult on everyone, but she was too young to realize how deeply it was affecting her. In the ensuing years her mother and sister gave her tremendous emotional support, for they were a loving family of three. But the hurt of growing up without a father caused deep wounds that would take her years to sort out.

In junior high she heard the message of Jesus' love for her, and she was touched; she even made a commitment to follow Christ. But her commitment, however important to her at the time, soon became a distant, though fond, memory. Her interest in Christ was sincere, but because of her need to control her life and her ability to cover her insecurities with her performance, her faith had little impact on her life.

When she turned sixteen, she decided that it was time to grow up and make her mark in the world. The path she chose was to control her environment in such a way that no one would be able to hurt her. She was strong, attractive, and gifted, and so she was successful at everything she did. She performed beautifully, without revealing to anyone the cause of her need to control. She was quite skilled at concealing her pain, even from herself.

Though she couldn't see it at the time, the relationships she had with men were attempts to make up for the loss of her father. She wanted intimacy, yet she also maintained enough distance to stay in control. She fell in love, but was not quite willing to risk, so she moved on.

During the next few years she made new friends and tried many different experiences, some more destructive than others. Life was to be lived, she felt, though in her heart she knew that her zest for life was nothing more than a search for the love and security she so deeply craved. Soon another man entered her life, and this time she felt she had met the answer to her deepest longings. She fell in love again.

A quick, fiery romance soon heated into an engagement. The girl, now a woman, allowed herself to let down and take a chance. Her fiancé was strong, intelligent, and handsome. He was the first man she had ever allowed to have such power over her. When he broke up with her, she was devastated. Her greatest fear had come true—all her life she had held on to the need to control her destiny, for in the loneliness of a fatherless childhood she had silently vowed to protect herself.

During the days and weeks that followed, in her weakness she sensed the Lord in a new way—He seemed to be hounding her, never quite letting her forget He was there. She found her Bible, and she read. The more she read, the softer her heart became. It was painful, but also bittersweet, for deep inside she knew that she was on the road back home.

She found a few friends who told her of the tenderness of God toward her, no matter what she had done or how she had lived. Slowly she began to see how she had been hiding behind her looks, her ability to control her environment, and her strength. She discovered how badly she wanted to simply be herself, letting go of the effort to be polished and protected in order to be loved. And she soon learned that because God loved her and was willing and able to protect her, she could risk her heart in relationships.

A little over a year later this woman became my wife. God has used Dee more than anyone else to teach me the meaning of living in response to grace. She still has lessons to learn, and hidden places of control where she occasionally retreats when frightened or attacked. But Dee's willingness to place all of her pain, background, security, beauty, relationships, and gifts at the feet of Jesus Christ, and trust in His great favor for her, is a wonder to see. I have grown because I have seen the great courage that Dee has shown, when she could have stayed in hiding for a lifetime, wallowing in self-pity or crushing others with the strength of her control.

Dee is a new woman who is actively going after what really matters: the deepening of a trusting relationship with Jesus. It has been hard at times, for anyone who honestly seeks to know Christ will be faced with the stark reality of the dark side of human nature.

If we are willing to let God take our broken and fragile spirits and create in us a new heart, we will be more able to live in freedom from the need to perform.

Is your journey any different from this struggle to turn away from self and toward God? In one way or another, we all travel this same path. Throughout our lives we have known little but the pressure to perform. Sometimes we may have felt ahead of the game, proud of ourselves as we whizzed by those who were struggling. But there have been more times than we care to remember when we were the ones left behind—crying, pleading, and trying to hide our wounds.

But the older we get, the more difficult the road of self-protection, and the easier it becomes to fall behind. So we try to run faster but just get more and more tired, more and more disillusioned. Then we finally notice that those who once were leading the pack have also begun to fall off and crash, one by one. A divorce here, a nervous breakdown there. We are all struggling.

In that season of emptiness and defeat, we have all but ignored the invasion of creation by the King who cares. God has heard our cry, and He has come with an intense compassion and a reckless commitment to pull us out of the kingdom of self, of darkness, and of lostness, and to bring us home to the Kingdom of God. His love for us is encouraging, passionate, tender, and extravagant. His call is to let go of our deepest need to perform for identity and accolades and trust *Him* with every broken piece of our heart.

Once we begin listening to grace, we are no longer doomed to the frantic search for the answer to the question, "Who am I?" He has given us a new name: "You are My beloved child!"

The choice in carrying on the fight of freedom is surprisingly clear and painfully simple: Do we trust Him enough to grab on to Him as He takes us into the wild unknown, or are we so tied to our need for performance and control that we will cling desperately to the reins of our lives?

In C. S. Lewis' series *The Chronicles of Narnia,* we see a portrayal of Jesus Christ in the great lion Aslan, lord of the land of Narnia. One of the residents, Mr. Beaver, tries to describe Aslan to a visitor to Narnia, a little girl named Lucy. After his explanation, Lucy asks, "Is he safe?"

"Haven't you been listening to me?" cries Mr. Beaver. "'Course he isn't safe; he's the King, I tell you! But . . . he's good!"[1]

Mike Yaconelli had these reflections upon turning fifty:

I look once again at the disturbed dirt of my life. I stare at the leaves of the past and *my heartbeat quickens! I can see something! I can see the tracks of God!* I am not very close, but I am closer! I am not there, but I know there *is* a there!

So here I stand, looking at the ground, smelling the faint fragrance of God. Never once did it occur to me that when I found God's trail again, it would ruin my life forever—for once you feel the breath of God on your skin, you can never turn back, you can never settle for what was, you can only move on recklessly, with abandon, your heart filled with fear, your ears ringing with the constant whisper, "Fear not."

Once you find where the trail is, you are faced with a sobering truth—in order to go on, you must let go of what brought you here. You *cannot* go on without turning your back on what brought you to this place.[2]

The only thing keeping you from knowing the freedom, joy, and peace of responding to Him with abandonment and following Him as King is the nagging sense of self-doubt caused by sin and the illusion of the performance ethic. Let it go. It has no real power over you. Trust the King to teach you how to respond freely to His love. In this you will find life, and life to the fullest!

As my four-year-old daughter proclaimed to Dee and me one morning: "How do you climb a mountain? Take one step at a time."

May God bless you as you walk with the One who loves you—one step at a time!

NOTES

Chapter 1—"I've Been Had!"

1. Today I understand and basically agree with the theology of "immersion" baptism over against the "sprinkling" of an infant, though it is not quite as cut and dried a biblical argument as I was led to believe as an enthusiastic sixteen-year-old.
2. Sue Monk Kidd, *When the Heart Waits* (San Francisco: Harper & Row, 1990), page 185.
3. Thanks to my friend Duffy Robbins of Eastern College for helping me to recall this experience, which is similar to his.

Chapter 2—In the Name of Love

1. In *Freedom from the Performance Trap*, David A. Seamands states, "Sloppy agape is a sentimentalized version of God's love which is so out of balance it excludes all the other aspects of God's nature" (Wheaton, IL: Victor Books, 1988), page 74.

In my view agape does not "exclude" other aspects; it overshadows them. There is no such thing as "sloppy agape," only the misunderstood or rejected love of God.

2. Steve Brown, *God's Reluctant Servant*, audiotape of presentation through Key Life Ministry, Key Biscayne, Florida.

3. Quoted in David I. Grossvogel, *Dear Ann Landers* (Contemporary Books, 1987).

4. Although for years I had assumed this poem was written by Renee's father, it was not original. He can't remember where he saw it, and during that crisis the words touched him so deeply that he had them written down and framed. The father's name remains our secret, by his request.

Chapter 3—"If They Could See Me Now"

1. Cited in the *Milwaukee Journal*, 4 February 1990.

2. Mike Yaconelli, in a keynote address at the Youth Specialties' National Resource Seminar for Youth Workers, spring 1992. His sources for the material in this quoted excerpt are as follows: James Patterson and Peter Kim, *The Day America Told the Truth* (New York: Prentice Hall Press), page 52; the *Denver Post*, 20 December 1991.

3. Thomas Merton, *The Hidden Ground of Love*, ed. William H. Shannon (New York: Farrar, Strauss, and Giroux; 1986), page 112.

4. Donald McCullough, *Waking from the American Dream* (Downers Grove, IL: InterVarsity, 1988), pages 26-27.

5. Robert S. McGee, *The Search For Significance* (Houston, TX: Rapha Publishing, 1990), pages 43-44.

Chapter 4—Trust and Obey

1. Bruce Theilman, "Bearing and Sharing," audiotape of a sermon presented to Glendale Presbyterian

Church in Glendale, California, date unknown.
2. Max E. Anders, *Thirty Days to Understanding the Christian Life* (Brentwood, TN: Wolgemuth and Hyatt, 1990), page 268.

Chapter 5—The "Blaming" Syndrome—"It's Not My Fault!"
1. Tim Larimer, "Dysfunction Junction," *USA Weekend*, 8-10 May 1992, page 6.
2. Quoted by Larimer, page 6.
3. Quoted by Larimer, page 6.
4. Quoted by Larimer, page 6.

Chapter 6—"I Did It My Way": The Deity of Loneliness
1. For obvious reasons, I have not used Mary's real name. This letter was recently published in my book for young people, *Next Time I Fall in Love Journal* (Grand Rapids: Zondervan, 1991), and is used by permission.
2. David W. Smith, *The Friendless American Male* (Ventura, CA: Regal Books, 1983), page 29.
3. Henri J. M. Nouwen, *Circles of Love*, ed. John Garvey (London: Darton, Longman and Todd, 1988), page 26.

Chapter 9—What Does Grace Look Like?
1. See 1 Timothy, where Paul instructs Timothy to "use a little wine because of your stomach and your frequent illnesses."

Chapter 10—What Must I Do to Be Saved?
1. Max DePree, *Leadership Is an Art* (New York: Dell Publishing, 1989), page 66.

Chapter 11—What Do I Believe?
1. Sue Monk Kidd, *When the Heart Waits* (San Francisco: Harper & Row, 1990), page 54.

2. Most of this material is a compilation of Henri J. M. Nouwen's writings, especially *In the Name of Jesus* (New York: Crossroads, 1988), as well as times of teaching and private conversation with him and Sue Mostellar, his partner. Dee and I are deeply indebted to both Henri and Sue for all they have given to us.

Chapter 12—Responding to God's Love in My Faith

1. Dallas Willard, *The Spirit of the Disciplines* (San Francisco: HarperSanFrancisco, 1988), pages 22-23.
2. Mother Teresa, *A Gift For God*, quoted in *A Guide to Prayer for Ministers and Other Servants*, pages 233-334.
3. Henri J. M. Nouwen, "The Struggle to Pray," in *Circles of Love*, ed. John Garvey (London: Darton, Longman and Todd, 1988), page 12.
4. Willard, page 185.
5. Eugene Peterson, *Reversed Thunder* (San Francisco: Harper & Row, 1988), page 93.
6. Abraham Joshua Heschel, *God in Search of Man*, quoted in *A Guide to Prayer for Ministers and Other Servants*, page 35.
7. Robert S. McGee, *The Search for Significance* (Waco, TX: Word, Inc., 1990), page xi.
8. Peterson, page 93.
9. Annie Dillard, quoted in *People of the Truth*, ed. Robert E. Webber and Rodney Clapp (San Francisco: Harper & Row, 1988), pages 68-69.
10. A. W. Tozer, *Pursuit of God* (Camp Hill, PA: Christian Publications, Inc., 1982), pages 81, 116.
11. Willard, page 182.
12. Willard, page 183.

Chapter 13—Responding to God's Love in My Family

1. Earl Palmer, *Alive from the Center* (Waco, TX: Word, 1982), pages 39-40.

2. Jerry Cook, *Love, Acceptance, and Forgiveness* (Ventura, CA: Regal Books, 1979), page 11.
3. From a poll cited in *USA Today*, 5 August 1988.
4. Cited in a review of Willard R. Espy's *The Word's Gotten Out* (Crown, 1989) in *The New York Times Book Review*, 7 January 1990.

Chapter 14—Responding to God's Love in My Friendships

1. Henri J. M. Nouwen, *Primacy of the Heart* (Madison, WI: St. Benedict Center, 1988), page 46.

Chapter 15—Responding to God's Love in the Tasks of Life

1. Henri J. M. Nouwen, *Life of the Beloved* (New York: Crossroad, 1992), pages 49-50.
2. Nouwen, pages 49-50.
3. Oswald Chambers, *My Utmost for His Highest* (Grand Rapids, MI: Discovery House, 1935), page 186.

Chapter 16—Carrying on the Fight of Freedom

1. C. S. Lewis, *The Lion, the Witch and the Wardrobe* (New York: Collier Books, 1950), page 64.
2. Mike Yaconelli, "The Terror of Inbetweenness," *The Door*, no. 126, November/December 1992, page 36.

AUTHOR

Chap Clark is the director of Youth Ministries at Denver Seminary, is an Associate Staff of Youth Specialties, and is on the Young Life staff in the Training Department. He has both a Master of Arts and a Master of Divinity degree from Fuller Seminary. A well-known speaker and writer in youth and family ministry, Chap has written several books, including *Next Time I Fall in Love,* a book for adolescents on healthy relationships, and *Let Me Ask You This: Conversations That Draw Couples Closer,* coauthored with his wife, Dee.

Why I Sponsor A Child Through Compassion

I can't think of anything more important in life than helping make an impact on the world in which we live by sponsoring a child.

Our family has sponsored a child with Compassion International for a number of years. That support of $24 a month - just 80 cents a day - covers the cost for Yudecka

Chap Clark

Maria Lopez, our sponsored child, to continue in school, have health care, food, clothing, and Christian training. Our entire family looks forward to receiving Yudecka's letters and we hope to visit her some day.

Compassion is committed to working through Christian partners in 23 countries around the world. They seek to minister to the whole person, and are committed to giving each child the best possible start in life...and the opportunity to receive new life in Jesus Christ.

You, too, can sponsor a needy boy or girl who needs love, protection, and encouragement.

By joining me as a sponsor, you'll receive your child's photo and personal story. You will be able to exchange letters and even send a small amount for gifts on birthdays and at Christmas. Your child will know you by name and appreciate your commitment of love and prayer.

Please join with me in giving a needy child like Yudecka a new start today by completing this coupon and mailing it to Compassion or by calling Compassion's toll-free number, 1-800-336-7676.

Yes. I want to give hope to a child who needs me.

My preference is ☐ Boy ☐ Girl ☐ Either
From: ☐ Any ☐ Africa ☐ Asia ☐ Latin America ☐ Caribbean ☐ USA*

Please select a child for my consideration and send me his/her photo, case history, and a complete sponsorship packet.

If I wish to begin immediately, I will enclose my first sponsorship check, indicating the amount here:
☐ $24 (one month) ☐ $72 (three months)

Name_____

Address_____

City_____ State_____ Zip_____

Phone_____ Age_____

Sponsorship is tax deductible and receipts will be sent.
*Sponsorship of a USA child costs $48/month, all other countries $24/month.

ECFA CHARTER MEMBER

C✺MPASSION
INTERNATIONAL
3955 Cragwood Drive
P.O. Box 7000
Colorado Springs, CO 80933
TOLL FREE: 1-800-336-7676
CC-B193

BUSINESS REPLY MAIL
First Class Permit No. 166 Colorado Springs, CO

Postage will be paid by addressee

COMPASSION INTERNATIONAL
3955 Cragwood Drive, P.O. Box 7000
Colorado Springs, CO 80933-9849